MAKING
A DIFFERENCE

MAKING
A DIFFERENCE

How one New Zealander created
a global business, and his thoughts
on the country's direction

Owen Glenn

with Michael Larsen

RANDOM HOUSE
NEW ZEALAND

Special thanks to Michael Larsen

A RANDOM HOUSE BOOK published by Random House New Zealand
18 Poland Road, Glenfield, Auckland, New Zealand

For more information about our titles go to www.randomhouse.co.nz

A catalogue record for this book is available from the National Library of
New Zealand

Random House New Zealand is part of the Random House Group
New York   London   Sydney   Auckland   Delhi   Johannesburg

First published 2012. Reprinted 2012.

© 2012 Owen Glenn

The moral rights of the author have been asserted

ISBN 978 1 86979 964 9
eISBN 978 1 86979 965 6

Text design: Megan van Staden
Cover design: Carla Sy
Cover photograph: Jane Ussher

Printed in New Zealand by Printlink

This publication is printed on paper pulp sourced from sustainably grown
and managed forests, using Elemental Chlorine Free (EFC) bleaching, and
printed with 100% vegetable-based inks.

Also available as an eBook

I would like to dedicate this book to my loving parents, Owen and Decima Glenn.

The proceeds of this book will go to the Glenn Family Foundation
to assist us further with the work we do globally:
Helping individuals build better lives and in doing so
strengthening their communities
www.glennfamilyfoundation.org

FOREWORD

What on earth is a dyslexic butcher supposed to say in a foreword to a book about Owen Glenn? Owen is a multi-millionaire businessman who built a network of hugely successful companies that he then sold, while I am just a humble working class lad from Newtown in Wellington who made a few bob with a chain of butchery stores and some cracking sausages.

But the truth is I had never heard of Owen Glenn until one day when the America's Cup was in town and I visited the Viaduct to take a peep at the super yachts. Just like the rest of the country, I was fascinated by how the other half live. Then I got chatting to a bloke about one particular boat moored there that day and he told me the one I was admiring belonged to a bloke from Mount Roskill.

For those of you who are not familiar with Auckland, Mount

Roskill is not the sort of suburb you associate with super yachts. And then this chap told me something even more interesting. It was owned by a man called Owen Glenn, and the day before he had taken a group of sick kids for a bit of a ride out on the harbour.

That didn't seem like something your average super yacht owner would get up to, and I was taken by the story, so I checked this Owen Glenn fella out. Turns out he was very far from a 'silver spoon in the mouth' rich kid with all the toys and trappings of wealth.

Certainly he was not short of a bob or two, but his story was compelling for many more reasons than that. Born in Calcutta, he arrived in New Zealand in 1952 with his family, going on to attend everyday schools like Balmoral Intermediate and Mt Roskill Grammar. He went on to be a bank teller, worked for what was then TEAL – now called Air New Zealand – and ended up doing the same thing young Kiwis still do, going on his big OE.

I won't pretend to understand all the business adventures he got up to, but it's safe to say he was no mug, and he ended up involved with a global logistics company, before setting up a Sydney-based freight company called Pacific Forwarding, and eventually going on to head DCL, Direct Container Line, which was so successful that US President Ronald Reagan gave it an award.

While I was chopping chops in Mangere he was being named the United States Entrepreneur of the Year and creating the OTS Logistics Group, which is the organisation bought up in 2012 by the London-based private equity group Man Capital.

In other words, this bloke Owen Glenn was the ultimate self-made man.

But while all this was going on, he didn't put the cash under the mattress and indulge himself with a flash new car every five minutes. He set about forming the Owen Glenn Foundation and finding ways to make the money work for other people, and always those with fewer advantages in life than himself.

To be fair, I would only do him a disservice if I tried to list what he has done for others, because the list is so long that I'd almost certainly leave something important out. Safe to say he supports hundreds of causes around the world. He is the person they invented the word philanthropist for. His donations to the University of Auckland's School of Business are well-documented. They tell me the $7.5 million he handed over is the largest private donation in New Zealand educational history.

But what really struck me was his response at the time of the devastating Christchurch earthquakes. In he stepped, unprompted, and donated $1 million. I still have a newspaper clipping of what he said at time: 'I grew up in New Zealand, it holds a special place in my heart and to see such devastation, such hurt and such loss makes you want to help. This donation is something I can do and I strongly urge other expatriate business people to do the same. We all need to pull together and while we are a small country, it is a country made up of people with huge hearts. That's what gets you through in times like this.'

Now let's be fair, New Zealand is a tough place, and we have a reputation for knocking tall poppies down, but I have only ever heard good things about Owen Glenn.

I finally got to know him a little better when he bought into the Vodafone Warriors, and I was often asked at the time what I thought about that. The answer was simple. I was delighted. Why wouldn't you be? Here was a self-made man with enormous intelligence, integrity and business acumen opting to throw his lot in with a bunch of working class people who love the great game of rugby league.

He even turned up at the official opening of my museum in Manurewa, where a big collection of sporting memorabilia is on show, and queued up like the rest of the fans for his sausage off the barbecue.

I do not believe for one minute that Owen Glenn needs the endorsement of a meat man like me, but I was very proud to be asked to write these words, because he is a truly unselfish and giving man. And frankly, there are not enough of them around. In fact I would go so far as to pay him the ultimate working class butcher accolade: He's not a bad bloke.

I hope you enjoy his story. My book *What A Ride Mate: The Life and Times of the Mad Butcher* got translated into Braille, which I remain very proud of.

So he might have the super yacht and own a chunk of the Vodafone Warriors, but he's got a way to go yet. Tell you what Owen, when this one gets a Braille edition, I'll do you a barbecue of your own so you don't have to stand in line.

Sir Peter Charles Leitch KNZM, QSM
The Mad Butcher

(For anyone who lives overseas, Sir Peter Leitch is an iconic New Zealander who, aside from being a successful businessman in his own right, is incredibly generous philanthropically, particularly with his time. He is loved by New Zealanders young and old.)

> *Grow old along with me The best is yet to be. The last of life, for which the first was made: Our times are in His hand.*

— Robert Browning

CONTENTS

"

People keep asking me, 'You had no tertiary education, you had no model to follow, you had no mentors, how did you do it?'

"

INTRODUCTION

LOOKING IN THE MIRROR, TESTING MY MORTALITY.

I ask myself a lot of questions. All the time. I can go to bed thinking one way on a problem and wake up with a completely different perspective. So I'm always checking in, if you like. And one of the questions I've had to ask myself a lot over the past year is: What do I want from this book?

Well, I want to make sure people are entertained. Anything but dull was the brief I gave myself. I want themes and stories that will be of interest to people rather than just a chronological sequence of events. The trouble is there's just so much that has happened in my life that I'm always thinking, Oh did I mention that? What about the time when . . .? During the whole writing process there was a little warning bell constantly going off, 'Owen, are you really going to convey things that might interest people?'

Because, despite being the story of my life, this book is, strangely, not just about that. It's also about how I express the experiences and the feelings that I have, and the convictions I've come up with. It was very hard in my mind to encapsulate all that into something that might be readable, but I've never turned down a challenge yet, and I'm hoping I've succeeded at least on that count.

To sum up my life? I feel I'm a bit like a travel writer who has a lot of fun.

The other night the wife of one of my friends, a guy who I've known for 40 years, said to me, 'Owen, I never stop wanting to listen to what you have to say because every time I ask something, you come back with an answer that totally surprises me. You always have a different perspective.'

I was quite taken aback by her comment and asked what she was talking about.

And she said, 'Okay, what do you think about the latest attempt by the Chinese to buy the Crafar dairy farms?'

And I said, 'Well, as long as we have reciprocal rights and we're in a global economy and we want preferred trade conditions, we have to entertain that.' Then I added, 'We can't ignore the fact that 1.5 billion people are just north of us.'

And she said, 'Why should we feel threatened about that? What would you recommend I tell my children?'

And I said, 'Get them to learn Mandarin.'

She looked at me and said, 'Well, I tried to learn Mandarin and I just couldn't do it.'

I said, 'That's two of us.'

Look, I hope I don't sound like a know-it-all. That's not me and I would be cautious of that. I put an opinion out there if I feel strongly about something and I'll back that opinion up, but I make no claim to have an understanding of everything. That's God's job.

There's the spiritual side of me which is the fact I believe there is a God. I believe we're all here for a reason and that's one of the reasons why I want to help my fellow man. It's ingrained in me. It's in my heart. It's just something I do. I wonder why other people don't do it.

There is the business side of me, too, which we show in here. That was extremely hard yakka, extremely hard.

Looking back over it all, which I now have the luxury of doing, I often say I've had seven phases of my life to date:

1. 1940–61

My formative years beginning in India to the age of 11 and then in New Zealand to age 21.

2. 1961–66

My OE to Europe and back in New Zealand.

3. 1967–69

Working in Australia.

4. 1969–80

The period I had in England and then back living in Australia for five years.

5. The early 1980s

When I went to the States and really advanced the business.

6. 1985–2000

A period of rapid expansion of my business.

7. 2001 to the present

Leaving the US in 2003 and relocating myself to, literally, wherever.

I see those periods of my life as times when my outlook changed, when I developed my self-reliance while having to cope with a lot of personal stuff. And there was a lot of personal stuff. I'm sure no one wants to hear me whinge about my problems, but I need to touch on them to complete the picture.

Then there are the trials and tribulations of setting up a highly complex business in almost all countries of the world and in all languages with all the tax regulations and so forth that I had to deal with. I had no backing and no money, and literally formed a personal cult around myself to develop a business that had no model to follow. People keep asking me, 'You had no tertiary education, you had no model to follow, you had no mentors, how did you do it?' Then they make the observation, 'I wonder why *I* didn't do it.' A lot of people have asked me that question, journalists who wanted to know the so-called secret of my success. That I think is important. There is no simple solution. There's not a list of steps that you have to follow; it's interpreting shifts in the currents and shifts in the winds and getting up each morning and looking at yourself in the mirror and asking youself, What I am going to achieve today? (I love that expression, it comes from Steve Jobs.)

People then ask, 'When you built all this up and it was all you, why would you want to sell it?' Good question.

Then there are the various personal challenges I have faced down, particularly in relationships. My mother told me in no uncertain terms that while I was an astute businessman, I was lousy at relationships. Looking back now, I guess my life's path has borne that out. What it came down to, and probably both my ex-wives may have to agree on this point, was the reality that on both occasions we simply weren't compatible. While there are two sides to every story, I was upset and amazed by some of their actions. When I lost my children because of decisions by the court it absolutely ripped my guts out. Despite an ability to focus on a whole lot of things at once, to not let outside circumstances distract me, those personal hurts started to consume me greatly, and not just while I was going through them. They depressed me hugely at the time and they still have the power to upset me if I spend too much time dwelling on them. Certainly, the relationships with my children could've been better.

I don't want to say anything to hurt my children now, so, out of respect for their feelings, and because it truly is history and a history that's best left alone, I won't get into the details. I'm gratified to say that in two instances I can think of, which I refer to later, the men got justice concerning access to their children.

I never hid my natural tendency to work hard, not from anyone. With my first marriage, I was working five jobs when we'd just had our first child Susan, *because I had to*. We were living in a state house in Otara and we'd had to borrow money just to get some basic appliances. I wanted better things for my family. I was always, always driven by a desire to provide a better life for my kids. Yes, I worked very hard and, yes, I enjoyed my work. But it was never just for me. And I did what I could. I would have to say that my counterbalance to the unhappy relationships was that drive I talk about, to provide, and to be successful. What also offset the bitterness and heartache of those years was the love of my children, the friendships I had with my mates, my involvement in sports and my success in business. At the end of the day, I *am* a family man, though: I have a family whom I love very much and I do my very best to look after them.

So there's a theme through this. Why would someone bother recommending this book? Why would that person say, 'You should really have a read of Owen Glenn's autobiography'?

In answer to this quandary:

I've passed the age of 70 and I'm facing a new era.

I've cashed out of my global business.

I've been in philanthropy for some time, over 32 years, and I believe that this is where my destiny lies.

What I look forward to more than ever are the intellectual challenges I'm facing.

I like teaching when I'm allowed to.

I like making speeches.

I like expressing my opinion, when it is sought.

As I face this new stage, more than ever, I need to stimulate my life by mixing with intellectually challenging people and projects, such as my association with the University of Auckland and my philanthropic work in Macau, China and India.

Having worked and lived in numerous countries over the past five decades I have found it incredibly difficult to maintain relationships at the level I would ideally have liked, so my close friendships are very important to me. I left people in Australia when I moved to the States. Those people, apart from one or two, are no longer in business — they've retired. The people I met when I lived in the States, they've gone because I no longer spend time in the States. Same with Europe. I suddenly woke up in the middle of the desert and said, 'Where the hell is everybody?' That's when I had to face what I am now and who

I am and what difference I can make. What do I really want to do? I've got a lot of drive and some mental capacity. So what challenges do I want to take on?

I hope that this book will answer some of these questions. Above all, as you make your way through it, I hope you learn something — about people, about business, about the way, I believe, the world works. I hope you're entertained, that there are enough funny stories and anecdotes to keep it moving, that there is humility in the telling of my story.

Most of all, I hope you will agree that we all have an obligation to help those less fortunate than us and that there are plenty of opportunities to exercise that obligation *right now*. That no contribution, whether it be money, time or some other resource, is too small to give. That everything does count and that you can help make a difference.

"

You could say I had a sort of mixed background: I'd actually been to six different schools by the time I was 11.

"

CHAPTER 1—
A STRANGE BUT CIRCUITOUS HISTORY

THIS BLOKE WAS BORN CHEEK BY JOWL WITH THE SLUMS, BUT HIS FATHER SENT HIM TO THE BEST SCHOOLS AVAILABLE WHERE HE LIVED. THEN WHAT HAPPENED TO HIM?

I was born in Calcutta in 1940, a combination of time and place that was exciting, frightening and deplorable. India was in the grip of sectarian violence: anti-British to gain independence and then religious divisions, Hindu versus Muslim. People were having their throats cut then the corpses pushed down manholes, women were mutilated then slung between power lines with their hair tied to another's feet. This was in the street right outside our front door. Fortunately, we were sent away to school. It was the thing to do in India; you got sent to the hills because it got too hot on the plains.

I was popped around the Himalayas to all sorts of boarding schools from the tender age of seven. You could say I had a sort of mixed background: I'd actually been to six different schools by the time I was 11. They were all run by different people: Christian Brothers, nuns, whatever. I think it led to me not believing in nesting. My mother was very, very protective; my father more practical. I was really distraught. I can still remember crying all the way to Darjeeling. I believe it was wrong, psychologically wrong in my case, to be sent away at that early age. Maybe if I'd been eight or nine, the age when most kids go to boarding school, it might have been different but in my case it psychologically impacted on me.

I was raised Catholic, although my father wasn't a Catholic, he was Anglican. My mother had been put through a convent but had to leave because her remaining parent died when she was 16. My mother's sister, my Aunt Marion, was a lay teacher and she was at two of the schools my brother and I went to, to keep an eye on us. The schools were run by Catholic orders; in general it was the best schooling available, but a very strange environment because of the way I so intensely missed my parents.

There were some awful situations. I remember an instance when I was aged seven in a convent in Darjeeling. Because I missed my family so much, occasionally, I used to wet the bed. The Sisters' harsh solution was to stand you next to your bed and to drape the wet sheet over your head for half an hour. For a seven-year-old boy, in freezing conditions, that was shameful beyond measure. There's a lot of good in the Catholic Church but there's a lot of bad, too, and some of it borders on the sadistic.

I've done a huge amount of philanthropic work in Kalimpong, not far from some of the schools I attended, and a lot of the work I do is with various orders of the Catholic Church. These people are wonderful, committed to helping their fellows, and have shown me a different side to a religion and way of living that I thought fairly ill of when I was growing up.

When we came to New Zealand, I just fitted in. We carried on in the Catholic school system, possibly because of pressure from my Aunt Marion, possibly because my father thought that consistency was the best recipe. But we lived in Mt Eden, Auckland, and the nearest Catholic primary school was in Vermont Street in Ponsonby.

Bus trips far too arduous and lengthy to be taken by a kid my age were soon stopped when my father, seeing sense, relocated my brother and me to the closer and, educationally, just as sound, Balmoral Intermediate School, 10 minutes' walking distance from our house.

My father, Owen Arthur Glenn, was a fascinating man. I think it would be fair to say that he never achieved his full potential, something I, consciously or unconsciously, have fought to avoid in my own life. A calm, non-confrontational chap — it was once said of him that he suffered fools easily — he was also exceptionally intelligent. In his final year at high school in India, he sat the senior Cambridge entrance exams and got 100 per cent in the five subjects that he sat, all in maths and sciences. My father possessed a prodigious memory and could recite poems and Bible passages at will, and also harboured an encyclopaedic recollection of historical dates and events. One regret I have is that I didn't stick around to learn more from him — I went overseas at 21, and when I came back he had started his long slide into illness and, finally, death. In the end my father got very ill. He had cancer and was in hospital for nine months; they took a lung out and he never really recovered.

Balmoral Intermediate led to Mt Roskill Grammar. One thing I did get in India was a very good education and my educational level was far ahead of my peers, particularly in subjects such as mathematics, vocabulary and English composition. When I turned up at Balmoral Intermediate I skipped Form One and went directly to Form Two. When I started Form Three at Mt Roskill Grammar I was in the single figures, third or fourth in the class. To be honest, I didn't try very hard. It came naturally to me, I'm lucky enough to be able to say. Proper vocational guidance would have steered me to a more challenging curriculum.

I had an interesting experience in Form Four, one of those that, when you look back, calls you to question your own behaviour.

The assistant head asked me to stay after the class. He said, 'I'd like you to consider becoming a prefect.'

I looked at him and said, 'Me? I couldn't do that.'

And he said, 'Why?'

And I said, 'My mates wouldn't like it. I don't like dobbing in people.'

That's how naïve and stupid I was. I should've done it.

When I told my father he said, 'Oh son, you should've. He was singling you out as someone with leadership skills.'

He was right, but I couldn't see it like that at the time. At Mt Roskill the prefects considered themselves above the others and I wanted to be just one of the boys enjoying the camaraderie of being with my mates. When I returned as an old boy to address the school, I told the pupils of my error of judgement.

In business I always felt more comfortable first talking to my warehouse people. They'd tell me what was happening in the company. They always liked to see me.

They'd say, 'Hey boss.'

'How are things going, fellas?'

'Oh we're doing better now. We had a bit of a problem with the railyard but we fixed that.'

I don't have a superior bone in my body. I'm not that way inclined. I'm quite the opposite. I don't care if a person's pink, black or yellow, I don't care about their station in life. Relationships at all levels are equally important to me.

When they fired my mate from New Zealand Wallboards, I went out on strike. There was only one person on strike and that was me. The foreman couldn't stop laughing.

I said, 'I'm on strike.'

'*What?*'

'I'm on strike. They can't fire my mate, he didn't do anything wrong. It was just the manager wanting to bring a mate in.'

So the foreman went to the manager and said, 'Owen Glenn's on strike.'

And he said, 'Fire him as well.'

So I said, 'F**k you,' and went to the union organiser. He said, 'He can't do that to you as well, now we're all on strike.'

My mate was reinstated, so was I.

I was actually talking to the great-grandson of the owners recently, and I said, 'Your bloody company fired me once.'

He said very quickly, 'Owen, you probably deserved it.'

We had a good laugh together.

New Zealand Wallboards was one of the iconic New Zealand companies in the building industry, another good old family company. They made Gibraltar board. We used to work 12-hour shifts: one week, six days, 6am to 6pm, Monday to Saturday and the following week it was 6pm to 6am. It was hard yakka. That's what built the shoulders up. I was a skinny bugger before that.

All that aside, the point I'm trying to illustrate is I'm not entirely right wing. Whatever's fair. That's that. Unions have their role to play.

Back to school. I wasn't a terribly studious person but I passed School Certificate, that great educational marker of a bygone era, credibly. I got 240 out of 400. That's all I needed. My dear brother swotted until the dawn and got 249. There's a life lesson there: I put in just enough, I suppose. Even I was surprised I got 240, although my father thought I probably could've hit 300 if I'd knuckled down. I think it was always available up here in my head but I was just not motivated.

We had different teachers for different subjects. I didn't really have teachers who pushed me and when it came time to weigh up future options, they were very limited; there was simply no career guidance. There was no mentoring, so there was no attempt at discussing what I should do with my future, or any aptitude testing or anything of that nature. It was an indictment on the education system. In a way I stumbled upon education and mentors as I went along in life.

My brother left the year before I did. He went to the ANZ bank. When my turn came, my father said, 'Well, you could do worse than your brother, go and join the BNZ, that's a good address on your CV.'

There was no question that I could go back for Sixth Form, which was then called University Entrance. All this was what I call LBSL — life before student loans — and there was simply no money in the family.

I joined the bank and it was a job. It obviously wasn't very well paid but the best thing about the bank was the social life. I was in the main branch at BNZ Queen Street in Auckland and there were about 100-plus young men and women in our late teens and early twenties, and we all got together socially. These were the salad days when we drank lemonade, sang along to Elvis Presley, danced and played guitar.

Even then, though, even in the bank, I set my own standards. I started in postages and then I did remittances where you worked behind the tellers. Then I was transferred to Customs Street West where there were four tellers, and I had just turned 19 and was made head teller. We had big payrolls like the waterfront and I can say, hand on heart, in that bank — and I was there 15 months — I balanced every single day.

So life had deposited me, pardon the banking pun, at the BNZ, and by age 20, something inside of me said, 'Life is not going to be about being the teller at Kaukapakapa or Waikikamukau.' That was not me. I was due to be posted to the country, that's what the BNZ did. I offered to go to Fiji — having been up there on a hockey trip and dated a beautiful girl, Miss Hibiscus, there — but, funnily enough, the BNZ said I wasn't old enough! So what was a poor boy to do?

I still believed my elders were my betters and all those sorts of traditional, hierarchical views that can sometimes hold you back. So, if I was destined to be the teller in Kaukapakapa I would've been. But I rebelled against it. I decided to go and pit my wits against the world as I had nothing to lose; I didn't have a formal education. At a very early stage I realised I had enough of the gift of the gab to hold my own in a conversation. I can argue my case inoffensively and I think if there's any one talent I have, that's it.

So I decided to go overseas, and the OE then meant some very long boat trips. I wanted to go to London and I had three different guys who were going to travel with me and they all let me down for various reasons. They all, one by one, pulled out, either got the pressure on them or got cold feet. I was at the proverbial crossroads.

Now one day my dad and I were weeding the garden and he said, 'What are you going to do about this trip, son?'

And I said, 'Dad, it's a little disheartening.'

And he said, 'What do you really want to do?'

And I said, 'I really want to go.'

He said, 'Then go, but don't ever tell your mother I said that. Now pick up that weed over there.'

That was all he said. I never told my mother and peace reigned at home. To get together a travel fund I worked at labouring jobs in a wool store (Parnell), a timber yard and foundry (Morningside) and the foresaid wallboard factory (Mt Eden).

England, 1961. Wow. Met up with some Aussie mates, had a crazy time, not much else to report. Wine, women and song? Pretty much. But work, always work. I did fruit packing, I worked as a plumber, I even worked the elevator in Harrods before they put me in the butchery department. How'd that happen?!

We'd got jobs at Harrods over Christmas. I was driving the elevator that they used to handle the overflow of customers at that time of year, and it also happened to be the lift the department managers used to travel up to their private tearooms. I have always talked to everybody and I remember talking to a guy by the name of Ducket. He loved the Kiwis. He had been in the desert during World War II and he said, 'I made so many friends in the Long Range Desert Group (LRDG), Kiwis and Aussies. How long are you boys here for?' (There was an Aussie guy in the other lift from me.) I said, 'Well, we're going to travel around Europe.' And he said, 'When this job finishes up, come and see me.' He gave me a job in butchery.

I didn't last long as a butcher. They gave me four sacks of loins to cut up for the staff lunch and the master butcher said once, 'This is how you do it,' and that was staff training! Well, there was a complaint after lunch, bone shrapnel in their loin chops.

When I was working as a cashier, I remember a woman, a duchess of some sort with a whole lot of bags, said to me, 'Can you help me to take this out, young man, my car's waiting.'

'Not a problem.' I carried her bags out, was chatting away to her and a Rolls pulled up. She got in and took out half a crown to give to me.

I said, 'Oh no ma'am, I'm a New Zealander, we don't accept tips.'

'Oh fine,' she said. 'That's refreshing. Thank you very much, you're a lovely young man.'

When I went back inside the guy on the door said, 'What the f**k are you doing?'

And I said, naturally, 'What's your problem?'

To which he replied, 'That's how we make a living.'

I said, 'Well, I don't take tips, learn to live with it.'

He reported me to the management. I was told that's the way it works.

I said, 'Look, I just did it for another human being. What should I have done, told her to carry the bags herself? Should I have taken the money and given it to the doorman?'

Management replied, 'Well, that's the way it works here.'

We all had to meet in the same place to put our uniforms on, and after that, they wouldn't talk to me, none of those guys. Ex-guardsmen, six foot something. I didn't care. Live your life your way, mate, if you want to end up as professional beggars.

My Aussie mates used to drag me away. 'Owen, stop it, they're big bastards.'

I got by okay. In fact, I had a great time in Europe.

One particular place in Europe, I remember fondly, was a beach in Monte Carlo harbour in Monaco. There are some large rocks there that form a breakwater between the actual harbour and the open sea. And, at one stage of my trek through Europe with my mates, we threw our sleeping bags down on those rocks and slept the sleep of the just. We had a visit from the long arm of the law but when we did our best naïve Kiwi-boys-on-tour routine — 'We've got no place to stay, sir, and we're only dossing down for the night' — he kindly went on his way. I remember it so well, I think, because about 40 years later I was back in the same city, with the task of presenting a cheque to Mikhail Gorbachev and his Green Cross International organisation. Staying in the opulent and ornate Hôtel de Paris, on arrival in my room, I pulled back the heavy drapes and, scanning the beautiful vista, my eyes caught sight of those same rocks. I remembered a young Owen George Glenn, back then with just £20 to his name, and then thought of what I was about to do, have a meeting with a man who had changed history, and I thought, What a strange but circuitous history I've had.

So much has happened since that innocent night with a bunch of blokes, yet parts of me are still the same guy: I still hugely value camaraderie; I have the same ambition and desire in me to taste the world as I did then; and I have a deep and ongoing love of the sea.

Something really big happened to me on that trip, which was that I grew up. I'd had to be self-reliant; all the things an OE should teach you. I had to find work, I had to find accommodation, all off my own bat. I had to keep mateships going, get on with all sorts of people, handle all sorts of situations. Travelling with people is a major test of any friendship, but I survived and flourished.

To prove just how much I value that camaraderie, I'll relate something that happened while we were in Europe. In Italy I met an American woman, married to a US soldier in camp there. For some reason or other she took a bit of a shine to me, and asked me if I wanted to go to see the running of the bulls at Pamplona. She had her own car, a Volkswagen. I wanted to stay with my mates, and told her so. I tried to put her off by saying I wanted to go to Paris — she offered to drive me there after Pamplona! Talk about persistent. And yet I still turned her down and stayed with my mates. Unbelievable but true: I was having such a good time with them. It might seem I'm not so good at relationships with females — I just don't understand women — but I stand firm and strong beside my mates.

That then was an exciting, motivating and critical period of my life but, eventually, I came back to New Zealand — mostly I just couldn't face another bitterly cold European winter. But I also knew it wouldn't be long until I was itching to get back up there, back to the northern hemisphere. However, events didn't quite pan out as I'd hoped.

The first thing I had to do once I was back on New Zealand soil was work out what I was going to do for a living. What was my career path to be? I'd been happy, up until that point, to go to the University of the Streets. Before leaving and when I was overseas I'd worked in a number of labouring jobs, as well as the brief stint as a butcher and the ups and downs of elevator work (!) as described above. I sat down and thought, I now know all the things that I *don't* want to do.

The only unifying theme I uncovered was that I really enjoyed travel. So I approached Air New Zealand who were, back then, Tasman Empire Airways Limited (TEAL). Just called them up and I got an appointment with the employment officer.

And he said, 'Why do you want to join TEAL?'

I said, 'I've done all these different jobs, sir, and I've figured out that the one thing I really like is travel.' I probably added, which is what I did think, that I wanted to start a career and I figured that the airline business was a growth business. Little did I know the impact that industry was going to have on the rest of my life.

He said, 'Fair enough, we'll give you a job.'

Just like that. I'm a firm believer in the phrase, If you don't ask, you don't get. I asked, and I got. I actually thought he'd say 'We'll keep you in mind,' but he said, 'Right, let's start you.'

There wasn't a specific job, right then, so they put me in as a trainee in their freight division, but those were the days when nobody knew anything about cargo. So I learned everything. I got every piece of paper I could get my hands on. By the time I'd been there six months they were all coming to me.

'Owen, what happens to this?'

'Oh that's class red, label B, you've got to do this and that.'

And so forth. I knew because I made it my business to know.

One thing that showed itself in my character at this time, which is 1964–65, was that I had a serious work ethic. Despite my lackadaisical efforts at school, where I did the bare minimum, I applied myself when it came to work. Later that was fuelled by having a young family to provide for, but I think that you either have a work ethic or you don't, and what I found out, when I started at TEAL, was that I most certainly did.

How did I end up with a young family? Blame my passion for hockey! One thing I had done when I got back to New Zealand was take up my interest in the sport and rejoined the Albertian Hockey Club and it was at a club party that I met a girl who was to become my first wife. Despite her swearing black and blue that she could never get pregnant I proved she could. And she did. We had very little in common but I knew the right thing to do was to stand by her, once pregnant, and support her.

It doesn't really matter now, but what it meant then was: Boom! All my dreams were shattered, this was totally unexpected.

We got married in 1964 and lasted together for fourteen years. In that time we had three beautiful children, Susan (1964), Jenny (1966) and Angela (1970). But outside of the children and my work, I would be lying if I said I was happy. When we got married I still owed £60 to the bank — I'd had to borrow money for the airfare home from the UK, as the agent over there with whom I'd lodged my return ticket had gone bust, another example of my naïvety. On my princely £12-a-week salary, I calculated we were already a year in debt.

I was nobody. I didn't own anything. We'd ended up living in Otara and once we'd had Susan we had to buy a fridge to keep the infant milk cold, and we didn't have any money. So I had to go to the BNZ where I had worked and a friend of mine had to guarantee me a loan for £100. That's how little clout I had anywhere. But the one thing I could do was work. So I worked, and hard. By the time I got married, I had five jobs.

I worked my full-time day job at TEAL, and did one night a week there, as well, at what was known as the bond store check, where we checked every piece of paper, every consignment notice, against every piece of freight. I worked Friday nights cleaning post offices and banks. I worked weekends at a service station on Mt Eden Road where I did everything — pumped petrol, sold stuff, changed tyres. My mates used to come around when I was working and talk to me. They came to keep me company, but they never helped, the bastards! But they'd come and ask how I was doing. Which was nice.

And every public holiday I worked at Ellerslie on the tote. Someone I had been talking to mentioned that the racecourse took on casual staff for race meetings so I went and saw them. That was great fun. It was a manual system back then, of course, and it was fantastic working out the odds and everything. Even so, despite my extensive involvement in the bloodstock industry now, back then it was just a means to an end: a way to make money to buy whatever we needed next — a cot, another baby blanket, some furniture. I was never driven by the money; I was driven by a desperate need to provide for my family.

These days you'd say, well, I have a mortgage to pay. Not back then: we got a house through what was called the State Advances Corporation. What a performance it was to even get that, a state house in Otara.

State houses were nearly impossible to get, yet I heard of people who had emigrated to New Zealand from England, got off the boat, gone straight to a state house which previously had been empty for six months. It wasn't right. So I assembled huge amounts of information. I talked about it to cab drivers. They'd say things like, 'A cousin of mine has a state house, got married to a guy and he has a state house so they both moved into the guy's house and they rent the other one. They're not supposed to.' Then they'd say, 'Do you want me to give you the information?' Sure I did. They'd tell me that the government couldn't do anything about scams like that, couldn't evict them. I couldn't believe it.

The Minister of Housing at the time had his constituency in Mt Eden, which happened to be where I lived. He actually used to play bowls with my dad. So I got all this information and, believe me, I went into this thoroughly. All the scams you could possibly imagine, people just completely abusing the privilege while others with a genuine need were missing out. And a government powerless, or, at the very least, unwilling, to do anything about it.

There was a Sunday paper at the time that just loved this sort of stuff. So I contacted the minister, John Rae, and said, 'I'm going to give all this information to them on Friday and it will be in Sunday's paper.' It was that well documented.

I had a call straight back: 'Come around to the State Advances office at 4pm.' And they gave me a key.

I went to the house and discovered that it had been vacant for eight months. Brand-new, just sitting there. The English bloke from State Advances, who came along once we were in the house just to see that I genuinely had a wife and baby, said to me, 'I only arrived just over a year ago and I was one of the people who came straight off the boat, got a key and went to a house.' He'd applied and got his house confirmed while he was still in England. While I'd been working my arse off here, battling away and paying taxes. Talk about a disconnect between government and people.

The sequel to all this was a letter from the Minister of Housing. It was a very short letter.

'I don't want you to feel that there was any [preference given to you] but perhaps you could just take note that your case was being looked at and did come up.'

Oh yeah: at 4pm on a Friday afternoon! I thought, Go and take a running jump.

So, while it was great to have a house, clearly the scheme, the whole process, was terribly flawed. So I did some thinking about how it could be improved, and I came back with a scheme. Back then, there was a system called Group Housing. If you could raise £750, that was all you needed to get a deposit on a simple house. They had all the plans, you could pick your design, a three-bedroom house, and you became the owner of that property. The government put the funding in apart from your £750 and you owed them at a very low rate of interest. It was reasonable in that you could put your time and effort and a little bit of resource in and keep the house tidy and the grounds tidy but it was your house. You would eventually own the house completely if you stayed in it or you could trade the equity in it. If you paid off half then you could move up to a better address.

I said to the government, to the Minister of Housing, in fact, 'Instead of letting people languish in these state houses, why don't you push them so that they can only stay in the state house for a certain number of years, say four, and force them to save through a scheme. Say they were staying there for £1.50 a week. Get them to pay £5, so £3.50 will build up and force them into a savings programme and within four years they could move out into a Group Housing place that would basically be their own home.' A sense of ownership, pride, that sort of thing. I never got an answer to that one.

And, as far as I can tell, the situation with state houses is exactly the same today. People have a very well-honed sense of entitlement and it's a total vote loser to turn the whole thing upside down and have a good look at it. There's simply no popular policy to vet the people on that entitlement. You could make a decision sitting in a village in Tonga that you're going to emigrate to New Zealand. It's a relatively easy process and you'd probably get into a state house within a year — from the time you decided to do that. Particularly with some of your family sponsoring you.

The whole system is in need of a serious audit on the

entitlement factors and the abuse that goes on. But where are the committed journalists who are prepared to dig a bit deeper and uncover the flaws in the system? Nobody is prepared or wants to take photographs and ask the questions, ask: Why are these people living here? How did they qualify for a house when these more suitable applicants have been on a waiting list for two years? Even if they are, no newspaper will be prepared to print it.

The entire thing caused me to lose faith in New Zealand; it was not just that the system was so horribly flawed, but that no one was prepared to do anything about it. I still remain concerned about the apathy and mediocrity in this country. We are capable of so much more and we should sort it out.

I had a house, then, but I was basically subsisting. I knew instinctively that Otara was a stepping stone for me. The way things were there, along with the housing system debacle, these were the two reasons that I decided I no longer wanted to live in New Zealand, certainly not a New Zealand that operated like that.

Another situation sealed it for me. There was a guy, he was a communist, his name was Somerville, and he ran the Hotel Workers' Union back then in 1963. He banned me from all the pubs in New Zealand. What on earth did I do to earn this privilege?

I'd been for a drink at De Brett's with a guy I worked with at TEAL. The guy I was with, Herman Tross, ended up, totally undeservedly, earning the wrath of the belligerent Aussie barman. The barman was drunk; Herman was the ex-heavyweight champion of the Dutch Army, a huge bloke. It was six-o'clock closing in those days, and you had until 6.15pm to finish your beer. it was 6.10pm, Herman put his pint to his lips and this little Aussie barman knocked it out of his hands, got it all over Herman. Herman rose to his full height, and this guy hit him. Extraordinary! We went up and lodged a complaint with the police at Princes Street. Next day, the cabin staff at TEAL were all threatening to walk out, because they were all part of the same union as the pub staff. I had a phone call from Wilson Whineray, who was the general manager of the brewery that owned De Brett's, and he arranged for us to meet this guy Somerville at the pub after closing. We turned up, he sat there and ate, refusing to acknowledge us. At 6.30pm I got up to walk out, and finally that got him going. He told us to drop all the charges, the barman was heading back to Australia anyway, it was all nonsense.

He said, 'I'm sure you see things my way.'

Herman said, 'No. No, I don't. I'm the injured party, that barman assaulted me.'

This guy started literally frothing at the mouth. Which is when he uttered the words, 'You two will never be served in a bar in New Zealand again. Ever.'

I said, 'Really? You really think you can do that?'

He said, 'Try me.'

I said, 'Okay. Tomorrow night I'm coming in to De Brett's to order a beer. You stop them serving me. And, by the way, I'm ringing all the press and asking them to be here. I'll see you tomorrow, pal.'

'Well.' He got all high and mighty. 'I'm not going to be here tomorrow.'

'Sorry to hear that,' I said. 'You're going to miss all the action.' I thought for a bit. 'What, do you have to go and hide somewhere?' God's sake, I was 23! Foolish! But I was incensed. I finished with, 'It's people like you who are going to bring this country down. But we won't let you.'

I said to Herman that I'd go all the way to whatever court he chose. I was the witness. I was prepared to see justice done. It was bullying: intimidation tactics. Ridiculous.

In the end, Herman was called in to the office of the general manager at TEAL, who said to him, 'Look mate, the union are going to close us down. If we can't get cabin crew, we can't fly.'

The barman, in the end, was tried *in absentia* and was, on paper, anyway, banned from ever returning to New Zealand, not that he would've. No one ever apologised to Herman. And that episode was one of the other reasons I left New Zealand.

For me personally, as far as my career was concerned, I saw TEAL as a launching pad, and that's exactly what it turned out to be. Within 16 months they'd put me on a course to learn ticketing and customer service with the intention of moving me to what they called traffic, which was reservations, bookings and everything that goes with that. I topped the class.

But a week after that I resigned because Emery Air Freight recruited me. Frankly, I liked TEAL, I liked it very much. I got on with all the staff there. The reason I went to Emery was because they gave me a car, a Commer Cob-Chrysler. Wheels! When you've just got married, with a kid on the way, your priorities change.

Emery Air Freight was a wonderful company, and I did everything there. I'd get up at dawn, head out to the airport and clear paperwork off the aircraft and check the freight. Then I'd race into the office in the city and work: sales, accounting, operations, whatever was required of me, whatever needed doing. It was hard work and poorly paid, and while the operations side was okay, the sales side was immensely difficult, airfreight then being a new, untested and obscure service that

New Zealand didn't seem quite ready for.

Tough times. I had this beautiful little girl that I had to look after and bring up, and I had lost control of my life. None of this had turned out as I'd expected, none of it was going in a direction that I wanted. I didn't have the choices that I'd had only a few years previous, when I'd come back from overseas. Not only did I feel trapped, I couldn't see any way out. I became flotsam and jetsam, totally at the mercy of the way the tides moved. I was hobbled. But I didn't give up. I refused to. What did I do?

I adapted. I had a job application for IBM, which I deliberately left in the glove box of my Emery company car so the boss would find it. I'd made it clear, then, that I wanted to go to Australia, that I needed something bigger, better. So they sent me to Emery in Sydney.

Because I was in the business, a good friend of mine at Pan American said to me, 'Owen, how much stuff have you got?'

'Not much.'

'We'll fly it all over for you.'

They flew it in the hold of a Pan Am 707. I just wrapped my stuff up in cardboard and string and they emptied every other piece of cargo out of the hold and put mine in. That's how I got all my stuff freighted for free.

I went over to Aussie with less than $100. I was in the depths of despair trying to see a future for myself but I was determined to do so. But it meant leaving my friends and family behind, a daunting memory for me.

"

I found the way to get ahead, to improve my circumstances, to start making decisions that might give me some choices, options.

"

CHAPTER 2 —
THE ODD STROKE OF GOOD LUCK

'WE'RE BRINGING UP THE ISSUE OF GLENN AGAIN.'

A ustralia, 1966. I had two children, one wife, and one job when I arrived in Sydney. I absolutely struggled to make ends meet. The Emery job was a better opportunity, but we were still living hand to mouth. I worked my arse off all the time. I remember our first Christmas there I couldn't afford to buy presents. I bought a stereo on time payment because it came with a hamper of goodies for free.

I'd had five jobs in New Zealand, so scaling back to one might sound like a holiday, but it was far from scaling back. The job at Emery was very, very busy. Work dominated my life again, although I did manage to get back into my sport, at least, when I was there. But I was still restless.

So I made opportunities for myself. I found the way to get ahead, to improve my circumstances, to start making decisions that might give me some choices, options. I just kept fitting myself in where I could. The breaks came and I took them.

I met with Harry Williams, then chairman of Australia's largest customs agents, Wathen, Curnow and Cox. He became very fond of me as I did of him. He was in his late sixties, a lovely man. He wasn't a mentor but he saw something in me and introduced me to other people.

It was Harry who gave me my actual introduction to what would eventually become McGregor Swire Air Services. It was then known simply as the Swire Group and had close ties to Ocean Transport & Trading in the UK. There was huge growth happening in airfreight and commercial services — this was the end of the 1960s — and both the Swire and Ocean groups had fledgling airfreight businesses. But they were, frankly, doing terribly.

Yet the industry was primed for growth. Sir Lindsay Alexander, chairman of Ocean, was visiting Australia and via an introduction from Harry, I met with him. I put a plan to Sir Lindsay that they should send me on a world trip to research the whole airfreight business, what was happening, what was likely to happen, and how they could get a piece of it. Five weeks later they approved my offer, and I left Emery, and Sydney, for the UK.

I arrived in England with almost nothing and I made something of it. I worked hard again. I saw opportunities. For whatever reason they took to me and used to call me The Antipodean. Success came later, and I built the business up into something quite extraordinary until company politics saw it all taken from me, cruelly. But it was quite a ride.

Initially, it all kind of stalled. I got put in a lovely office but wasn't really given anything much to do. After eight months I asked for a meeting with John and Adrian Swire and effectively said, 'I'm wasting my time and your money. I've got a young family, I may as well go back to Australia.'

That got a reaction. I was duly dispatched to Sir Lindsay in Liverpool and had to front up to him and 14 other directors and tell them why the airfreight business might be good for them. I was treated a little bit like the young upstart but, fortunately, both John Swire and Sir Lindsay had taken a bit of a shine to me. So I got my day in the sun and said my piece. I told them I had a 'ground floor' opinion of how they could better run their airfreight business. After that, another six weeks of nothing and then: Boom! They decided to set up a company: 70 per cent Ocean, 30 per cent Swire and while they wanted me effectively to run it, they felt that, at 29, I was a bit too young. So I recruited my previous boss from Emery to head it up and I ran under the title of director of marketing and agencies. I ran the company and its expansion, looking after, primarily, agency, sales and development. My family also came to live in the UK . . .

I had no management background *at all*. I had been a salesman and a sales manager. But I put together a business plan for them (it was terrible, but it was simple!) and I put together McGregor Swire Air Services (MSAS). I got them a licence into Japan, and we were the first non-Japanese non-American company to get a licence to fly freight out of Japan: it was quite an achievement. It had taken two years of extensive meetings and lobbying to convince the Japanese Government to issue export airfreight licences to any country outside of the US. It was a huge coup.

I went on a massive expansion programme, coupled with a comprehensive list of acquisitions, buying companies across the globe. I bought Dutch companies, Italian companies and American ones. There was one US company which was run by a typically flamboyant American. He was the whole nine yards: white shoes, candy-striped pants, bow tie. His ethics were as questionable as his dress sense.

We, MSAS, ended up in quite an argument with him over the value of his company. We'd bought into them because they gave us instant access to the US market and some serious volume. But this guy decided he wanted significantly more than what we thought he was worth, and really started talking up the 'intrinsic value' of what was, in fact, a totally unprofitable business. The Swire guys were getting very uncomfortable, and told me so.

'What do you think, Glenn?' I was asked.

'Well, sir, I think we should give Mr X his taxi fare to the airport — what do you think of that, Mr X?'

'I will sue you.'

I'd been expecting this. 'Let him,' I said. 'He hasn't got any money. And we can prove a number of other things which Mr X has been claiming as inconsistent.'

Silence.

He'd been asking US$6 million: we paid half that in the end.

This whole time was a huge learning curve and it really, really stretched my mental capacity. I had to make sense of concepts that, having left school at 15, I knew little about. Real seat of your pants stuff. In the end I had bought seven companies and had 1800 people working for me. I became the heart of the beast: it was an amazing time. Hectic, pressured, but amazing. And then it all fell over very, very quickly.

I should've known, really. I was told four years into MSAS that I'd never get the top job. They were that blatant about it. I hadn't gone to university. 'You're not from the same class.' That's what they said. I thought, You're kidding me.

But they weren't. They simply moved someone in, a relative of the chairman of OCL Containers — who, ironically, I had brought in from Ocean Group — and threw me out. He was first cousin to the MSAS chairman, who had been brought in because he himself was first cousin to somebody else. That's how it worked. They called it 'differing management styles'.

It was, ultimately, a bitter experience. I got over it, especially as I went on to become so successful without them. Despite them. But I had put my heart and soul into that company and that was the thanks I got.

I just didn't — and don't — believe in that 'born with a silver spoon' bullshit.

By 1974, I'd built the whole thing up, the networks, everything. These days you'd say it was my IP. That was my knowledge they sold.

I'll balance that by saying that it was really just that one guy who I had trouble with. MSAS management were my mates; a lot of them still are. He was just the guy at the top but nobody listened to him. What happened to him, incidentally, was that he was eventually transferred to a company in Singapore. The Singapore Government caught them out in a fraudulent deal to do with an acquisition of government-owned shipyards. He was fired and dismissed. I heard through the grapevine they made a substantial settlement on him.

Karma? I don't know. It is very strange. He went to Australia, we know that much, but nobody knows where he is and nobody has seen him. He doesn't contact anybody and they don't contact him. He was the rising star of the group.

The Swire Group opted out of MSAS management in favour of Ocean. The whole of Ocean, the mighty empire of Ocean Transport & Trading, was seven different shipping companies including these main ones: Blue Funnel, Glenline, Henderson Line, Elder Dempster. All these companies were sold off and transformed into Overseas Container Line (OCL) where Ocean took a 46 per cent interest. They had all sorts of trucking companies, aggregate companies and natural gas carriers, and all these companies eventually failed. Except one. MSAS. I believe they sold it to Exel and then to DHL for £6.5 billion. My baby. That's the truth. Isn't that amazing? The enterprise was a multi-generational family business which held the majority shares of the whole Ocean Group and they're the ones who in the end got the cash. Thanks to me.

At the time of my falling out with Ocean, I was on £6000

a year. I'd just been put up from £4500. That was slave labour. I argued with them because the guy they put on behind me in Australia, a guy called Robert John Rankin Delaney, was getting more than I was. I was basically the whole group and he was just Australia.

I said, 'I'm an expatriate from Australia, I should be on more than him.'

And they said, 'We don't recognise expatriates coming to Britain.'

Unbelievable.

That lot can go wherever they like in the world and be expatriates so I said, 'I eventually want to go home and live in Australia. You employed me in Australia. I at least have to keep pace with what I'd earn there.'

Swire went in to bat with Ocean for me, and as this disagreement went on they sent messages around on a silver plate with an envelope, and on the envelope was Ocean. So English! I read some of the letters and they went something like this:

> *Dear Lindsay,*
> *We're bringing up the issue of Glenn again.*
> *We don't believe you have treated him fairly,*
> *we'd like you to reconsider.*
> *Swire.*

This went backwards and forwards. They offered me three months' salary when they got rid of me, which was nothing. I ended up with two years. Which was still nothing! Twelve thousand pounds.

So I just said, 'Bugger the UK, we're going back.'

My wife at the time felt the same way. Even though she was English, I'd met her in New Zealand, and she loathed the cold in England. I knew I didn't want to go back to New Zealand; it was too small for me. But that's where she wanted to be, so I left her in New Zealand and went to Australia to look for work. I was 34. Suddenly I didn't have anything. I literally looked for a job as a salesman.

When I went over to Australia a pal of mine said I could stay at his place. So I did. I lived way down south of Sydney and had to get the train in to go to job interviews. I owned one suit. Two shirts. I had to hit the streets and get a job. There was nobody to help me. Even people I'd known five years previous weren't able to help. Back in 1975, Australia was in a bit of trouble, in the doldrums, and people just weren't hiring.

Before I left the UK, though, I'd already talked to a guy over there who was ex-TNT and so, when I got to Australia, I got a call from Ross Cribb, who was the right-hand man of Sir Peter Abeles, managing director of TNT.

He said, 'Owen, I heard you were coming back. Have you got any time to come and see us?'

'I think I can fit you in, Ross!'

I went to see them and they were in this large room: Sir Peter was in one corner and Ross was in the opposite corner, diagonally, and there was a phone on each desk. These two phones would just be ringing and ringing. They'd call Don Dick, TNT manager in New Zealand: 'Hey Don, Peter here, what have you done for the company today? How much money have you made for the company?'

This was how he talked. I loved it, still do. Great attitude.

So Ross Cribb said to me, 'Look, we're all over the world. We've got this in America, this in Canada, this in Singapore, this in London. How do we make money *in between*?'

And what he was really talking about was freight forwarding, my thing. I said, 'Well, I'll have to see what you've got.'

He said, quick as a flash, 'How long will you need?'

'Six months.'

'Fair enough.' He said, 'Do you want a title?'

I said, 'No, I don't think I need a title.'

And he liked that. I was just researching and putting it together and I needed to contact a lot of people on the phone.

Next thing he says, 'We'll send you to Hamilton.'

Hamilton was the guy's name, who was in charge of the international division. I thought he was a real piece of work and he didn't want me around from the start.

'We'll give you a desk and a chair and anything you need.'

And I said, 'I haven't got a car.'

Ross picked up the phone and said, 'I'm sending Owen down now, give him a Holden. Anything else?'

'Well, look, I've got this problem trying to get a mortgage because I haven't got a job. I've got enough of a deposit but I haven't got a job.'

He picked up the phone and rang another number, 'Look, we're putting on a young man here, Owen Glenn, mind if I send him down? He needs a mortgage.'

(All I had was the £12,000 that I'd been paid out by MSAS. Eventually I sold my house in Britain, but I had to wait nearly a year to do that because the housing market was so terrible. In the end, when my money came through, I reduced my mortgage and managed to put the kids in a good school.)

I sometimes wonder why Ross Cribb did all that for me, and can only put it down to the guy having a big heart. Big heart. So I went down to Martin Place, Commonwealth Bank, eighteenth floor, and saw the chief general manager.

'Ah Owen, come and sit down. How can we help you? When Rossy Cribb rings up, we're happy to help. What do you need? Oh that's not a problem, mate, we can rush those together for you. Who's your real estate broker? What's the pressure on you?'

'Oh, you know what they're like, got to close tomorrow.'

'Right, give me his name and number.' He rang the broker personally and said, 'We're giving Owen Glenn a mortgage for this much. This is my name, chief general manager . . .'

I can't tell you the relief.

So I did a study on the TNT business. Sir Peter set strict criteria on the report that he wanted done.

'Tell me on the first line how much money I'll make. Tell me on the second line how much money I need to invest. Tell me on the third line how long it will take. If I like those three numbers I will read the report. And the whole report should be done in two pages, no more.'

Great advice for report writers everywhere!

And I did it. That's exactly what I did. They then sent me to the Pilbara region in north-western Australia where they were thinking about doing other things. I didn't even know where it was. They said, 'We supply everything up there from Perth. We think we can do a lot better. You go and find out.'

I went up there, looked at everything, and put in a report about supply chain management. They read it and said, 'Fine. By the way, we've looked at your first report, and we want you to do it, set up a global freight-forwarding company.'

But of course I'd been considering all this. I said, 'Oh Mr Cribb, I've actually been thinking about this, I think I can do it myself.'

He said, 'Really? Great.'

I said, 'I'm going to have to borrow a couple of grand and I've got a partner called Malcolm Bush.' And that's exactly what we did. Good old Ross Cribb, though, he was so supportive. His final words to me at the time were, 'We're going to keep an eye on you to make sure we see what happens.' It was great of TNT to do that for me.

I saw him three years later coming through Sydney Airport and he came over and asked, 'How's it going, Owen? I've heard you're doing well now.'

He knew *everything*. I told him what I'd been doing, and he said, 'Wonderful. Well done mate, well done, we're proud of you.'

I replied, 'Thank you for giving me a wonderful start.'

It was quite a big decision to go out on my own. By then I had three kids and while my wife was worried — a lot — eventually they came and joined me from New Zealand.

I said to her, 'It's time, if I don't do it now I'll never do it.'

Because, the thing was, if I didn't go out on my own, what would I have done? I would've had to go into a completely new industry and do so as a salesman. I probably would've joined IBM. I nearly joined them in 1966 and this was now 1975.

The thing is, while I could have set up a global freight-forwarding company for TNT, I knew what to do anyway. And through my time building up MSAS, I had all the connections — people who had supported us and people who were competitors of ours, too.

So Mal Bush and I put in $3000 apiece, bought a couple

of second-hand Holdens, and Pacific Forwarding Group was born. I went about getting all these agencies that fed freight into Australia, because Australia and New Zealand were, and to a degree still are, such heavy importers of goods, and those key agencies were what got us started. But it was tough going. There were four of us in a tiny room just ringing and door-knocking, calling on every contact I had. I didn't have any money and I was working my arse off again. I was a salesman again and it was very hard, but we built it up, hand to mouth, and I kept it on an even keel. We put our houses up as collateral to get us some working capital. My connections with the overseas principals for the agencies we were handling meant we kept their money for 60–90 days, which gave us some cashflow.

We had the odd stroke of good luck. One example. Amatil, who owned Lucky Strike, wanted to make a denim cigarette packet — it was meant to be along some sort of cowboy theme, I believe. Their shipping was late so they asked us to fly all the material in to Australia for them. So we flew in some very light denim, which took up all the space on the aircraft. We made $12,000 on that job. When the broker gave me the $12,000 we celebrated. I gave half to Mal, who paid his kids' school fees and I took the other $6000 to my family. (The cigarette packets, incidentally, were a flash in the pan: never worked.)

Initially that's how we lived, by windfalls, until we built the customer base up by becoming the Australian agent for those international freight forwarders. With incoming freight, 75–80 per cent is 'collect', so the forwarders would prepay the airlines and the shipping companies, the freight would arrive, we'd collect all the money from the importers, which gave us cashflow, and then we'd settle in 60 days what we owed the overseas principals.

Our big break came when containerisation took off from the United States into Australia. The Russians, Far East Services Company (FESCO), were running five ships, not very big ships, only 600 containers on board. But they were coming out of the United States at a rapid rate. Their guy, who was an American, Harry Malendy, got on very well with me. We did a great deal with them. However, our whole deal then collapsed due to President Carter withdrawing their licence over Russia's invasion of Afghanistan. On the last ship we had 76 containers on it and we made AUS$2000 a container. A bloody gold mine. We didn't lose the freight but we had to put it on other carriers without a special deal. These were the sorts of things we had to do to establish ourselves. Every moment, everybody we talked to, it was all part of making it work. It was a very high-energy period.

But the problem was, as we got successful, the agencies wanted to open up in Australia themselves. Profit Freight Systems, Forward Air, they all started establishing their own offices. Once we'd built the business up, they felt they no longer needed us. When that started happening, I knew that it was time to head back to the northern hemisphere.

So I opened up Direct Container Line (DCL) under the parent company Overseas Transport Services (OTS) in the United States. With $2000. *There it is, right there, the start of it all.* That $2000 is what I turned into a global success story. I was commuting across the Pacific, one minute loading containers in the US and the next back in Sydney running a board meeting. I'd go straight from the airport to a meeting of supporters, freight forwarders, customers, and I knew I couldn't keep it going for too long. You actually get quite exhausted. Everywhere you went they offered you a drink, which didn't help at all. I lived through all that and that's when I wondered, Where does my future lie? I said to Malcolm, my business partner, 'I can't do all this.'

I knew I had to get back to the northern hemisphere. So I was in the States with my two employees but I could see the future.

Bless him, and we're still good mates, but in my opinion Malcolm wasn't a great businessman. I looked at the two companies we had — Pacific Forwarding in Australia and DCL in the US — and said to him: 'You can sell me both companies, you can buy both or you can take either one. What do you want to do?'

Malcolm couldn't get his mind around that so he kept the Australian one, the more established one. Then Malcolm went off and tied a deal with our competitors. There were three companies that had formed some sort of loose triumvirate in the States, and the guy I put in to help Malcolm, Bob Delaney, the same fellow I had left behind in Australia when I was at MSAS, in my opinion duped both Malcolm and me, by persuading Malcolm to break the contract with me and deal with our competitors. Mal needed to give me six months' notice but he didn't do it and it created absolute chaos.

I'd just been on a five-and-a-half-week business trip around Asia and had got back to LA when I heard the news. I went home, picked up fresh clothes, went back to the airport and left on the 11pm flight for Sydney that same day. When we landed, I had a huge attack of gout. I could hardly walk. Extreme pain. I went to the bank manager who I'd dealt with for years, but,

'Sorry Owen, you don't have any identity any more here in Australia as you no longer have a company.' He wouldn't give me an overdraft, wouldn't give me anything, wouldn't let me open an account at the Bank of New South Wales.

But I still had a business to run, DCL Australia. The choices were to work with an agent or open our own offices and I went with the latter. And the guy who helped me through all that was Harry Malendy, the one who I'd set up the FESCO deal with. Opal Maritime was their company in Sydney and their agent helped me out after Harry rang them up and said to look after me, that I was all right.

They gave me their boardroom and they allowed me to put phones in and I was employing people to sit around and do this and do that. We still had the volume, oodles of pouches coming in which had to be processed, and invoices raised. Those people, Opal, I owe a huge debt to. They all went home at 5pm and we were there until midnight. They let us stay in their office, which is really something. They gave us a key and we were in at 6am. And I just grew it from there.

How did I progress things? I moved on. And what I did in fact, all I did, really, was take the reasoning and the logic and the culture of airfreighting and apply it to shipping. I'm talking about the days when freight would get piled in a net on board the ship, the net would swing over to the dock and they'd drop it from 10 metres. They'd actually drop the net!

The wharfies would go, 'What's that? Let's take a couple of those . . .' It was in those days. And then I applied the same logic, the same principles to shipping in containers. I burrowed in very fast on that, using the knowledge from my airfreight days.

As for airfreight, as the aircraft got bigger and catered more for freight, business just started to boom. A lot of that had to do with approach, doing things the right way around. This time we went in and got the secured space and then we sold to that space. We didn't ring Avon and say, 'We can handle your freight to South America'; we said, 'We've got the space to handle a certain capacity.'

To build up to the level of a worldwide operator takes a lot of different things: understanding tax laws, setting up a company in a foreign country, making contacts in the various countries, hiring staff, setting up premises, arranging phone lines and furniture, knowing regulations for the physical loading of freight, etc. — all in different countries. You can't do it organically now, you've got to do it by acquisition. Now there are just so many more carriers, which is why it's important to secure your space before you offer it, before you sell it. There are simply too many big players, the German companies, all competing for that space.

Through the middle to the end of the seventies, my marriage was coming to a close and in 1978 my wife and I called it quits. The events surrounding that are typical of the misunderstandings and miscommunications that often are the hallmarks of disintegrating relationships. I'd been as involved in the lives of my daughters, Jen, Sue and Angie, as I could be.

We were engaged in what I would describe as a horrible custody battle and she argued for, among other things, the house and half of my business. I explained that the business wasn't worth a dime without me and that there was no way in the world I was going to effectively go and work for her. It was madness. I stuck to my guns until finally they agreed to take the house and leave me with the business. She got custody of the kids as well. Hardly a win-win as far as I was concerned.

Months later, in July 1978, I met my second wife to be and within six weeks had asked her to marry me. Talk about rebound! My parents expressed deep concerns about the decision, as they had with my first marriage, but I guess I just couldn't be told. Wife number two was an Australian who had walked out on a marriage in England and returned home, which would've been fine — I was hardly in a position to complain about her being divorced — only it turned out she wasn't entirely sure if she had officially terminated her marriage. Her 'walking out' meant just that — she had simply bolted from what she said was a marriage of convenience to placate her mother, but inconveniently for us, it began to appear as if, a week before our own nuptials, she had never actually got around to being legally divorced.

'I think I wrote and asked for an annulment but I don't know what happened,' she told me.

A good mate of mine in England raced up to the Leicester court where this had all (hopefully) happened, got proof of the annulment and sent it by courier to Australia, and it arrived on the eve of our wedding.

Perhaps I should've seen some warning signs!

"

We really had a field day on this one, and went on to become the market leader as a direct result of this initiative. My initiative!

"

CHAPTER 3 —
BEING TWO JUMPS AHEAD

WHY WAS IT SO SUCCESSFUL? IT JUST HAPPENED.

W hen I first went to the United States in 1978 and launched DCL, I did so, as I mentioned, with only $2000. I used to go in on tourist visas — I actually set up and ran the business from 1978 through to 1986 initially on just tourist visas and at the end on a business visa. I never had a US driving licence. And, of course, I couldn't open a US bank account.

I had the most bizarre experience with a bank when I was

trying to get some bridging capital.

I went to this American bank and said, 'I just need some working capital.'

The manager looked at me — and I'll never forget this — and said, 'Well, Mr Glenn, how much do you need?'

I said, 'Three hundred thousand. And I want it on overdraft on a call basis.'

And he said, 'Well, you put $300,000 in a certificate deposit with us and we'll lend it back to you.'

I said, 'I beg your pardon? If I had the $300,000 why would I ask you for it?'

Honest to God that's what he said. I just gave up on that and obviously found other ways to survive. Later on in life they were lining up at my door but I didn't need them.

By 1980 wife number two and I had moved from Australia to Los Angeles so I could better helm DCL. At this stage, despite the horrendous court battle for custody of the children from my first marriage, my first wife had thrown the two younger kids out and they came to live with me. Two guys I've already mentioned, Bob Delaney and Mal Bush, went round and picked up the two girls from the neighbour's; that's how literally they'd been thrown out. Sue, fortunately for her, was on a course in England at the time; Jen and Ang came to live with us in Palos Verdes, California.

The problems began immediately. Not with me and the kids — I loved having them there — but with wife number two and her sister, who in my opinion was incredibly unfair and mean to them. She basically didn't want them around.

As far as she was concerned, they were old enough to go their own way. Sadly, they did. Angie went back to school in

Sydney, as did Jenny for a bit, but then she returned to do a teaching course in LA. She was completely ostracised by wife number two, so I got her her own apartment, which helped things all round.

This, again, saw difficult personal problems proving to be an unwelcome distraction from what was becoming a rapidly flourishing business. I was lonely, too. My parents, of whom I was so fond, were back in New Zealand, thousands of kilometres away. I'd left some great friends in New Zealand and England when I exited MSAS. I'd made business acquaintances, but little more, in the States and home life was difficult as I tried to look after my family.

We spent some time living in London during this period, and had also bought a place in Australia, an isolated but beautiful home in the Belrose area near Manly in north Sydney. It was during this period, the mid-1980s, that I'd been getting in and out of the States on a range of visas, as I've said. I actually entered the United States 28 times before I got a B1 and B2 visa, let alone a Green Card. In the end, the only way I got in permanently was via my wife who, being born in Australia, had been able to attain a residency visa. I went in as her husband. (Being born in India was of no use to me; India had zero allocation of visas or applications for residency.) It meant that I had to arrive and be resident in the US on 1 January 1986. It cleared up all the complications I'd been going through, continually applying for different ways to come and go and, crucially, from a business perspective, it allowed me to form a Chapter S corporation, which had some distinct tax advantages. In short, these allowed me to preserve personal income and defer taxation payments, a very beneficial prospect at that stage of the business. This was one of the ups I was able to use to my advantage; hold on for long enough, though, and you get to weather a few downs as well.

So how did I manage to crack America, and the world? With honesty and integrity intact.

There are so many stories that come to mind, looking back, that were deciding moments in the course of my career. At the time, they just seemed to be the next right thing to do. By the early 1980s I'd really started to consolidate (!) a great business in the ocean freight industry. Airfreight really sparked in the 1960s and 1970s, and it took off when the bigger jets came in, the 747s and so on.

The 747s had started running down from the States to the South Pacific when I was with Emery. Then, in London, MSAS were very keen to get into both the Australian and the American markets. However, these were dominated by four American companies. So I went to see British Overseas Airways Corporation (BOAC) in North America; they were based in Park Avenue, New York. The cargo manager's name was Colin Marshall, the very one who ended up as *Sir* Colin Marshall, the chairman of BOAC. And if anyone wants to challenge the veracity of this story, or thinks it's just another of Owen's anecdotes, I have it on very good authority that Sir Colin still tells this story himself.

I would've been 31 at the time I went to see him. He knew my reputation because Emery was the top forwarder in the Australasian market and I'd done a lot to build it up both in New Zealand and Australia. The way the market stood at that time, BOAC used VC10s for this sector, which had holds you had to crawl into. Pan Am, Qantas and so forth were using 747s, where you slid the freight in on the containers.

I simply said to him, 'Colin (I might've called him Mr Marshall), we can't get into this market.' Then I asked him, 'How much do you handle down in Australia?'

The response was, 'Very little, we haven't got the right equipment.'

I said, 'How much capacity do you have?' Although I already knew all the answers before I asked him!

He said, 'I don't even know.'

'So, how much revenue do you make?'

He said, 'I know that! Bugger all, $160,000 a year or something.'

Now I knew that if they actually filled the holds, that is maximised their capacity on every flight, they could be earning $1.6 million. I told him this.

He said, 'Yes, but we can't carry the containers.'

So, effectively, they couldn't compete due to the specifications of their aircraft. The main freight companies wouldn't use his aircraft because they got better rates in the container; the container space was about 30 per cent cheaper per kilo than hand-loading in a VC10 because of the handling. He wasn't competing; he couldn't. He couldn't handle anything big because it couldn't fit in the hold.

Because of these limitations I saw an opportunity to bring the price down. I said to him, 'One hundred and sixty thousand a year.' Pause. 'What if I guaranteed you $320,000, double what you make, and you give me all the belly space every day. I'll buy it all off you. Win, lose or draw.'

He said, 'I like the sound of that.'

I said, 'Now, as I'm sure you understand, all these other guys, these other freight companies, are going to dump on you.' These were what I called the Big Four: Airborne, Emery, Air Express International and Circle.

But he was smart. He said, 'Look Owen, they need me before I need them. If they want to move their freight on BOAC flights to and from Europe and they give me a hard time then they won't get the space. No aircraft, no airfreight. I'm not even worried about North America to Australia.'

He agreed to it and I signed the contract with him. I actually did it at his desk. I wrote it out. At that meeting. He signed it and he said BOAC will honour this. We ravaged the industry.

He wasn't going anywhere with that space, but I knew how I could use it. What we did was target all the commodities businesses. We went to the right people in those industries and we cut the rates, I think by 28 per cent if I remember correctly, lower than what the big boys were charging in the containers. He put no constraints on me whatsoever with pricing because, simple economics, he wasn't getting any of the business anyway. All hell broke loose.

All the other airlines screamed and yelled, but he just said, 'Well, I've got to run a VC10 every day.' He didn't tell them what I was paying him, but said that those big freight companies could offer the same if they chose. Of course they didn't, because they had been making such a huge amount of money off their clients, charging a premium to freight in containers. We were happy making $20 a kilo and they had been making US$50. If they matched us they would've lost. The freight companies immediately put the pressure on Pan Am and

Qantas and the others to drop their rates in the containers but they wouldn't do it. Do you know why? *Because they were the only game in town.* They didn't have to. This was before FedEx and DHL and courier carriers. These guys, Emery, Airborne, they had nowhere else to go. Which is not a good place for a freight company to be! We really had a field day on this one, and went on to become the market leader as a direct result of this initiative. *My* initiative!

Another initiative that proved to be ground-breaking caught the rising wave of the technology sector, at the beginning of the 1970s. A good friend and colleague of mine, Bob Hackett, once wrote that I started the 'Silicon Valley to Singapore return' business. Now that might be a bit generous, although it was certainly my idea to put together what would become another one of those career-defining moments, a decision and action that had huge implications for — and a large and positive impact on — my business.

Where to begin? The airfreight business is very time sensitive, and delays can be hugely expensive. None more so than in the computer business, which was just starting to take off on the west coast of the US. If a small part breaks down and the computer stops, that costs hundreds of thousands of dollars an hour in lost time. Now, the circuit boards for computers were being completed back in the east and were being flown over by the US-based Silicon Valley companies as normal freight, over Tokyo, over Hong Kong. It was airfreight but it took five to seven days for the entire round trip. Again, that was about one operator having dominance, having control. In those days, Cathay Pacific would only go to Hong Kong — they didn't go direct to Singapore — so the freight would have to change planes in Hong Kong and Tokyo. Then Japan Airlines would take the circuit boards on to Singapore. Messy, complicated, costly and time consuming. These computer companies literally had production lines in Singapore, with people sitting there waiting with soldering irons. It was unbelievable.

The guys handling the cargo made it worse; too many people in the chain. The US cargo controllers of Japan Airlines would argue with the Japanese cargo guys; finding space on connecting flights was a nightmare.

We were doing some of this business. From memory we had a little bit from three customers and there were eight big players. I thought, Okay, what can we do here? There's got to be a better way. So I consolidated all of the freight and moved to a freighter that flew direct to Singapore. All the traffic managers, even though they were in direct competition with each other, and all knew each other, could see that this was going to solve the headache. They phoned their clients and said, 'Talk to Bob Hackett, he's got a great idea here.'

What sold them was the transit time. Including the turnaround, I figured — and was proved right — that we could go up Thursday and be back Sunday night. When I sold this to clients they didn't believe me. But we did it.

We'd load up, fly direct, land, unload. The production line would work all night on the boards and we'd load them back on the next morning. Because of the time factor, the boards came out of the States on a Thursday night and went back ready for action Sunday evening. The momentum built when we proved the speed of the service along the lines that we got direct space going into Singapore. We absolutely cleaned up.

But what's worth mentioning is that I took a huge risk. We started this venture on a commercial aircraft but I went into it on the basis of the knowledge I had of what was coming, which was that a freighter was going to be in service in three months' time from when I started pitching this. So I went out gangbusters against the horizon date. I went to the carrier concerned and said that we'd block off a substantial part of the aircraft, a guarantee to them that we'd fill the space. They were absolutely chuffed that someone would take half the aircraft. It made the whole venture successful for them. So that all helped. While it started on commercial, when it swung to a freighter, we had the box seat. We actually destroyed all the competition. We came up with the idea and so all these clients basically got rid of their favourite freight forwarder. They had to go where the action was, go with who was more aware of what was happening.

And the beauty of it was that we got these companies worldwide. They gave us all their freight. Our sales just rocketed up. It was at the birth of technology; it was just the right time. That's where I believe I'm blessed: I just *knew* what was going to happen to the technology industry, and I knew we had a way we could fix their main problem.

One thing about being in business for any length of time is that you get to experience the full economic cycle, boom to bust and back again. You can prepare for that. What throws lots of businesses are the unexpected events, things like the 1987 stockmarket crash, the 2008 economic meltdown and the terrible events of September 11.

The impact of the Twin Towers was in every conceivable way massive. On a personal scale, a national scale, an international scale. In terms of business: trade stopped dead. Just like that. And I had to downsize. It took me four to six months to get to the point I was comfortable operating at and, of course, in my business, where there's no asset base, it was all to do with downsizing people.

There literally was no business, it just stopped. But overheads kept running and revenue ceased, so hard decisions had to be made. In my type of business you can contract and expand as long as you protect the margins. I asked all my executives to take a pay cut and they all did.

I said, 'Look guys, it's either that or I have to let some of you go and that is extremely painful for me.'

And they all looked at each other and said, 'No, that's fair enough, Owen. We'll ride it with you.'

So that loyalty started way back, with the good attitudes they had. Consequently, I paid them back handsomely when fortunes turned.

Those downturns were out of my control, but were, as I say, manageable in my type of business. But if I had had a business buried in debt and with assets I would have gone bust. A working factory becomes a stack of bricks.

But to keep going, keep the momentum going, keep the image that you're surviving when everyone else around you is falling over is extremely difficult. I was in charge of everything, really, except for the PR and the announcements; even during difficult times I had to keep dispensing hope. You are relied on to communicate things like, 'There's an end to the cycle' or 'We'll be taking this action'. Though I must admit there were many, many hours when I sat on my own in the middle of the night, looking over the lights of LA, thinking, Christ, how do we meet the payroll? Those were dark and gloomy days but we survived.

My second wife had walked out on the marriage in the early 1980s, returning to Sydney, pausing only to clear out the bank accounts in the process. When I was down in Sydney on business not long afterwards, she informed me she was pregnant. With the benefit of hindsight, the situation might look complicated and fraught with poor decisions, but my options at that stage were to leave her, pregnant with our child, to fend for herself, or to take her back. Not much to think about, really. Personally, things took a brighter turn when Michelle, my fourth daughter, arrived in June 1982. Well, that was a highlight; everywhere else personally, it was, as they say, going to hell in a hand basket.

In an incredible feat of déjà vu, she walked out of the marriage again, this time during my father's seventieth birthday celebrations in Auckland, and, when I caught up with her at her mother's in Sydney, once again she told me she was pregnant. The outcome of that was my daughter Catherine, who was born in 1984. In 1985 we returned to the Belrose property to live and Christopher was born in that year. So by the time we returned to the US in 1986 for me to take up as a 'proper' resident, we now had three children in tow. Never do anything by halves! Things would turn tumultuous in the marriage — which ended in another bitter custody battle where, again, I lost my children. During this period, I also had some battles to fight on the business front.

By the mid-1980s, going into the 1990s, American wharfies basically held the shipping lines in a state of anarchy. When containerisation came in, the waterfront unions, led by an Australian by the way, had these huge salary demands, extortionate, in my view. At the time these guys were already getting over $100,000 a year in an era when $30,000 a year was considered a good wage in the United States. They'd have four people loading and unloading a single container, plus a forklift driver and foreman. Anybody in the terminal whose first language wasn't English had an interpreter. So, being America, you'd invariably have a Polish guy, a Hungarian guy and a Spanish guy, and they'd all have interpreters who sat in a special office and read magazines. What the shipping lines charged to load and unload a container was astronomical and all they did was pass that on in rates to the shipper or importer.

Then we came along, completely unaware of all this. We were what is known as a non-vessel operating common carrier — an NVOCC. Basically, it meant that we weren't a shipping line or airline: we didn't own our own vessels. We simply booked space and moved freight. The upsides of that model were manifold, the obvious one being we didn't own any major assets. Didn't need to. More on that later.

The way it worked was that we'd sign a contract with the shipping company, who within the contract would provide the container, and we'd send our truck along to pick up the box or however many boxes we were loading from a client, take it back to our warehouse and load it in a container using the same two guys who were also driving the forklifts. We didn't need a translator, for starters! And we did it three or four times faster than your standard wharfies.

It's worth mentioning that while this was going on in the States, there was a very similar mentality in New Zealand for a long time. With everything that's gone down with the recent Ports of Auckland dispute, some might say it still exists. I remember a funny situation when I operated in Wellington; it would be cheaper for me to send two of my loaders from Sydney on an aircraft than use local labour. Coming in on a morning flight, they could have unloaded two or three containers and gone back on the evening flight to Sydney for cheaper. That's how bad it was here.

Back to my situation in the States. What happened is the unions went on strike over this: they didn't want us to be able to load the containers. We fought, and the carriers fought them alongside us because they were trying to break the back of the unions. The courts intervened and ruled that the union's jurisdiction would be restricted to 50 miles from the port. This is what became known as the 50 Mile Rule, and everything that went on around it became a very defining time in my career.

Technically, then, we were not allowed to load shipping company containers; otherwise the wharfies, under advisement from the union, would refuse to load the ship. I love challenges like this, because I have to go away and think. Which I did, and figured out that in this case if we leased the containers ourselves, we wouldn't need shipping company containers and the unions would have no right or leverage with the shipping companies.

We simply said, 'They don't own the containers, we're not giving them back their containers.' What worked for us was that under the law an NVOCC is both a shipper and carrier. We were carrier in our relationship to the owner of the goods and a shipper in our relationship with the shipping lines.

This sort of posturing and behaviour affected our business in all sorts of ways. I had to constantly be two jumps ahead, constantly thinking of ways around actions that were being taken that negatively impacted my business. For example, we did business moving freight into South Africa. We ended up in a situation where we couldn't get the shipping company to bring the containers we were using back to the States because they were ultra-sensitive about offending the unions. So we ended up with a whole bunch of containers down there that we had leased and were paying a per diem cost. So I flew down to South Africa, did a deal with one of the mining companies, sold them the containers, which they were going to convert into bunkrooms. So they cut out doors and windows, put in air-conditioning units, bunk beds and toilets, and now all these mines have got my old containers as accommodation!

But it just shows you what we had to do to survive. This union battle raged for 13 years, and for us it got worse. The same carriers who eventually made peace with the unions, an uneasy peace but peace all the same, then turned on us and didn't want us around any more. So they used their very, very strong lobbyists to try to write us out of the Shipping Act so we would not have any support. They did it twice and our attorney, Ray de Member, who used to be with the Federal Maritime Commission (FMC), and still had contacts there, was being told by them: 'There's a major problem here, Ray. You've got to come and address the situation.' Both times he came in at the eleventh hour with the staying order signed by a judge. We were that close to going out of business. Just like that! Overnight! Boom! Gone! Thank you, Ray de Member (now deceased).

We eventually won — it went all the way to the Supreme

Court and it came down in our favour. For me, that still wasn't enough: these guys had done everything they possibly could to ruin us, and I wasn't going to just walk away from it.

So I was in a meeting, the union lawyers were there, and I said: 'Right, now it's our turn. We're going to file a suit for damages.'

And this guy said, 'Well, Mr Glenn, let me explain something to you.' This is never a good start to a conversation. He went on, 'We're going to subpoena every piece of paper that we think has had any bearing on this case over the past 13 years. We're going to subpoena bits of paper that you should have and you haven't got. We're going to fill up warehouses. You are going to spend every cent you have and you know who is going to pay for this, Mr Glenn?'

And I said, 'No.'

He said, 'The shipping lines. The same ones you've just won the Supreme Court order against.' And he added, 'They will just put it on the rates, American shippers and importers will pay for it and we will destroy you.'

I said three words, 'God bless America!' And walked out.

We didn't sue and they didn't do anything. I had to personally write off $1.3 million. We had no choice. It would have taken up thousands of hours of my time. Depositions, arguments for and against. If I'd pursued it we wouldn't have survived. It's like 'The Gambler': you need to know when to leave. They were perilous days.

The result of all this is that it's now written in the Shipping Act, the revision of the Shipping Act in 1984. It's now considered in the American public interest that the NVOCCs are part of the maritime industry. They can never move us out. It was a bittersweet moment; character building, as they say.

What surprised me was how truly horrible some of the people involved were: sleazy lawyers, people who broke their word, people who were lying and in the halls of power. Now, I'm not completely naïve, but people who were given positions of trust for their supposed integrity out-and-out lied. Threats were made. Incredible underhand stuff.

You had to really know your stuff, have done all your homework as well as keeping as current as possible with what was happening in the industry, especially in a legislative sense. And, even then, the powers that be could throw in a complete curveball.

I recall the time I was fighting the FMC about rebates and their lawyer said to me: 'Mr Glenn, you need to remember that the United States Federal Maritime Commission controls the rates going outbound — to anywhere.'

We were operating in South America at that point, and it meant that we had to file our rates from the US to Chile, which was technically okay. Our company in Chile — a separate company to DCL which was registered in the British Virgin Islands and so had nothing to do with the States — did a deal with a terminal there to unpack our containers. Once the shipment leaves the United States the FMC has no more control over it. When it arrived in Chile our office directed our trucks to deliver the container to this terminal, which happened to be owned by the same parent company that ran Chile Line. They did a deal with that company locally which was a very good deal for us, and it gave us control.

Of course, somebody complained.

FMC said, 'Well, when you offer this rate you're getting a rebate back from the terminal.'

I said, 'But that's a matter between our Chile office and that company, which is a separate company, the Chilean one. It just happens to have the same parent.'

They insisted that was a rebate and contravened the laws of the United States. We argued fiercely that it didn't. I had to go and front up to their attorneys.

And this guy — his name was Glassberg — said, 'Mr Glenn, I've been the head attorney here for eight years and I've served another 30 years of service beyond that. And I'm actually retiring on 31 December. I've never lost a single case.' And then he went on, 'You may or may not know this, Mr Glenn, but the Congress of the United States does not support the Federal Maritime Commission. There is no subsidy from Congress. We have to make our own way, pay our own way with funds we collect.'

I said, 'Well, to me, this is simply an out-and-out case where you think something and I'm interpreting it another way. So, since we disagree on it, surely the Federal Maritime Commission, the six commissioners, should decide.'

He said, 'Well, if you want to take it to the commissioners that's up to you.' Pause. 'And they'll just toss it straight back to me.'

I said, 'Well, why don't we take it to a judge in a court?'

He said, 'I'm not inclined to do that. I'm on the verge of giving a stop order.' Which would have put us straight out of business.

And I said, 'Well, we'll fight it.'

He said, 'It will take you six months and you won't have any customers.'

And I burst into tears. I said, 'Excuse me,' and left the room. I went to the toilet, gargled and looked at my teeth and smiled.

In my absence, he said to my attorney, 'What the hell was all that about?'

He replied, 'Well, he's just going through a really bad divorce and his wife's being nasty.'

I went back in and apologised and said, 'Well, I'm sorry. I'm a bit on edge. I've really got a serious . . .'

He said, 'Your lawyer's just told us.' He continued, 'We always intended fining you seven figures and the figure we've come up with is $3.8 million.'

I said, 'Well, I might as well just send you the papers signifying my business is closing, because we haven't got that sort of money.'

He said, 'Well, Mr Glenn, I'll tell you what. In the next seven days you send me a copy of your divorce papers and if we believe you we will amend that figure.'

We sent them the divorce papers. They brought the fine down to $800,000. On top of that — and this was a significant factor, too — if you plead with them, as I did, and they say they will agree with what they call 'no contest', which they did, there will be nothing in the file about it; it will not be lodged as a guilty admission, just as no contest, and you agree to settle out of court. Win-win.

My personal life at this point, 1991, as is apparent from that story, was in disarray. The divorce from my second wife I can only describe as protracted, ugly and messy. My children moved to Santa Ynez, California, in what I think was, on her part, one of the most selfish acts I have ever witnessed. I rented a house in Palos Verdes and then bought one in Redondo Beach in an attempt to be at least geographically near them.

There were upsides to that dreadful year, though, one being that I graduated from the Owner/ President Management Program (OPM) at Harvard Business School, which was, to me, a huge achievement. Also, I received the honour of being named the (US) Entrepreneur of the Year at a black-tie bash at the Century Plaza Hotel in Los Angeles.

The business was accelerating, too — growing at 20–25 per cent a year. We grew through volume, and when that rationalised, we grew through my programme of acquisitions. I basically went out and bought up our competitors. As an organisation, we changed shape dramatically as a result, moving from being an entrepreneur-led company, to a national one, to a global corporation through to a multinational identity. Through all these changes of structure I had to learn different ways of controlling the growth, different ways of running the business and different ways of staying ahead of the game. Inevitably there were potential restrictions to our growth, and I really took on the role of opening up the world for NVOCCs. Korea and Brazil weren't quite ready for the plans of Owen George Glenn, I was to discover!

In fact, I was having a major problem getting into Korea. Korean NVOCCs could open up businesses in the US and compete against American companies, but US companies were forbidden from entering the Korean market. This didn't seem reasonable to me so I involved the FMC, with whom I had not that long ago crossed swords over the issues we were having with rebates in Chile. Chris Koch, who became a great friend, was chairman of the FMC. It appeared to me that the lawyers on the FMC were singularly protective of their jobs. The same FMC treated me appallingly. But Chris Koch was Chris Koch.

I said to him, 'You know, Chris, we cannot do business in Korea, but the Korean companies can come into the United States at their will.'

He told me to write a formal complaint to the commission, which I did. They called a meeting, made a decision, and advised the Korean Government that every Korean ship entering US waters from a certain date would be fined $100,000. Just like that. A huge move. That was almost a declaration of war. But FMC had the power to do it. To them, I was an American company. It didn't matter what nationality I was.

The Korean Secretary of Transport came to the States within five days and signed bilateral agreements allowing American companies to enter Korea. It was my action that got him there.

I had the same issues in Brazil. Brazil had a rule that anything shipping in and out of Brazil, 40 per cent had to go to Brazilian carriers, 40 per cent to American, 20 per cent to anybody else. They were protecting their interests. With the experience of Korea under my belt, I thought I'd try the same thing again. But this time, the State Department pulled on the brakes. They wanted to study the information. And study it, and study it.

Then, one of my contacts, a Harvard alumnus, somehow procured all the records of the Brazilian Maritime Authority (BMA) on the subject of allowing DCL to enter the Brazilian market. This guy was a lawyer and he actually sent me the entire file in Portuguese. They'd studied it all and they'd agreed not to do anything. I sent it to Chris Koch again, who rang the State Department. A month later NVOCCs were allowed in. They had said to the BMA, 'We'll stop every Brazilian ship entering American waters.'

I refuse to be told no.

When I wanted to get into the market in China, and my aim was to buy a Chinese company, I got told by government agencies in the US that they'd bring it up at their next bilateral discussion with the Chinese Government.

When nothing happened I wrote back and they replied, 'The agenda did not allow us enough time to address the subject, we'll bring it up at the next bilateral . . .' and the next and the next, and it would never, ever happen. But I kept writing. And by piling on pressure, we eventually got in. I bought Ocean World Shipping, the biggest company in China who did what we do. At the end of last year we had 28 offices in China. There is huge potential there; it's absolutely phenomenal.

But China is not the free ride to fame and fortune that so many people think it is. From a governmental point of view, very rarely can you bombard the Chinese or bully them. That wasn't the way. The way was to talk to them and suggest 'Why don't we do this?' The way it worked was that we had to be in partnership with a Chinese company; but there weren't enough Chinese companies, so the concept broke down. Our solution was to buy a Chinese company, which caused the Chinese Government to go through a real soul search. In the end, frankly, they couldn't find reasons not to let the deal go through.

Taiwan was a problem, with the same sorts of challenges as China, but the rest of South East Asia presented little or no barriers to entry. Japan caused us heartache because it's full of all the huge conglomerates that have a large presence in America and all over the world, so there was no one we could partner with that made very much sense. We went through a sequence of things, working initially with an agent and then setting up a small company and allying ourselves to a company called Sagawa, which is worth sidetracking on for a second.

I actually sold my company to Sagawa in the mid-1980s and then bought it back two years later. The original deal was that I got Sagawa an airfreight licence in Japan, something they desperately wanted and which I facilitated for them. In return they bought my company, DCL. I did it purely so they could secure the airfreight licence using DCL's worldwide footprint. They didn't have the expertise to run my company, and consequently they came to the conclusion they couldn't run the international seafreight business. They were a million miles from it! They were like couriers; their logo was a messenger carrying a load with a bamboo pole, which was more informative than it might at first look. Japan is hillsides, mostly steep hillsides! So, the truck would pull in and these guys would have to deliver running up and down stairs and around back alleys. Utterly inefficient. Labour intensive.

They knew NVOCC wasn't their business. They didn't know how to run it. So they gave the company back to me. I remember they sent a guy, head of Japan Air cargo in Hong Kong, to come to talk to me. This guy was probably 12 rungs under me, to be honest, and he could barely speak English. He came to LA and we went out for dinner, and he drank too much sake, found he couldn't understand anything and got frustrated. On this occasion we left the restaurant, got on to the footpath and he was going to take a swing at me.

We sorted that out and next morning he was very apologetic, as you'd expect, but I was pretty annoyed.

So I said to him, 'I'm thinking of reporting you to the chairman. I think you should recommend to your board, to Sagawa junior (who was the president), that you should sell this company back to me.' They approved it.

So then he met me in Hong Kong in a hotel. We were in my suite and I beat him down.

He said, 'Oh have headache, have to go down get painkillers.'

And I said, 'No, I'll have painkillers sent up.'

'Oh I have to go.'

'No, you're not leaving here, mate.'

I battered him down. 'Let's put all of this down on a piece of paper and you sign it.'

That's what happened. Then I went to Japan and they formally handed the company back to me in a great big ceremony. They had got their licence, I pocketed about $6 million and I got my company back.

I followed it up and the guy I had been dealing with just disappeared. Sagawa junior was demoted and given a very small prefecture in Tokyo to run. His cousin, Nakamura, who was the treasurer and Chairman Sagawa's nephew, was sent off to a farm. He could not get a job back in the industry. Nobody would employ him. The last I heard, about 10 years ago, he was still there. He liked it. In my opinion he was totally unsuited to finance.

Sagawa senior himself, I met only once; he was a very special guy. He befriended the Americans after the war and he set up a very small bicycle courier business in Osaka. You've got to admire the guy for having a vision like that. Think about it: look at the courier business now.

They were a very big company, very powerful, but they

were so naïve. They did the strangest things. I remember they set up business in France and wanted to have something there so they bought a château complete with moat and deer in the park, the whole nine yards. They did it up at great expense, all for the purpose of giving their people somewhere as a base to live while they learned about railroads and trucking in Europe. I actually went there once. They sent a whole team of people out from Paris, it was an hour-and-a-half drive from Paris, to open up the whole castle for me. They were like that. They took the National Noh Theatre to the Vatican to entertain the Pope. They did all sorts of things like that.

The story has a sobering ending: the Japanese tax department caught up with them and they're now a permanent fixture on the Japanese tax authority radar. They had to pay more than US$700 million in fines. Maybe they sold the château . . .

But the Asian philosophy, particularly when it comes to business, is just so different. The basic premise is that Asia is certainly a land of opportunity but each country is different, each family is different, and the Asian economy is very largely driven by family. And you need to remember there are 2000 people in a family. They give all their aspiring children the best educations they can anywhere in the world and they expect them to come back and serve the family or stay overseas and do the same. That is their strength. They will do deals if they like you and trust you.

Every territory is different from the other. India, for example, is full of corruption. Very difficult to get by there with your integrity intact. We resisted the corruption by dealing with an agent, getting a third party in there. I actually suspected at one stage that they were overcharging importers. Complaints came back to the shippers and they told us. So I wrote to the chairman, who's a former sea captain, and just said, 'Look mate, cool it. I don't want to have to take any formal action but just talk to your brother [head of pricing], and cool it. We can't have it. These are major freight forwarders who deal with us. It's almost bordering on extortion. Overcharging won't work, you'll force me to get rid of the agents and enter the market to deal with this.'

I've done this many times. It stops and then it starts again. I have always said I won't tolerate bribes or any form of corruption. Integrity is sometimes all you have left, and once it's gone you never get it back.

The freight industry underwent so many changes since I set up DCL. The reason we stayed in the game was because I built the business to keep expanding and evolving, to keep pace with an industry that was constantly changing. And I made it all happen with just $2000.

"

Professors loved doing this course with the entrepreneurs. They said that they learned more from us than we ever learned from them.

"

CHAPTER 4 —
GREATER CLARITY OF THOUGHT

'FIVE BILLION IS FIVE BILLION.'

One of the greatest joys of my life came as the decade turned from the 1980s to the 1990s. As mentioned earlier, I applied for and was accepted into the Harvard Business School's entrepreneurs' course, known as the Owner/President Management Program (OPM).

I believe now that you're better off completing a formal

education, then taking some time out and going and sowing some wild seeds, bouncing off a few walls for a while and then studying again, once you understand what you're looking for. I did it all in such a hurry, with a pregnant wife, in my early twenties, being forced to work at a whole lot of jobs just to keep us going. It meant I was learning everything myself, on the job, from what I could read when I had the time.

What influenced my decision to do the course was a conversation I had with a guy living in the US, an engineer: he'd done it and he told me about it. He urged me to go, yet I really didn't think I would be accepted. But he gave me all the information; you had to go through quite a lot just to apply. Harvard required that you present recommendation letters from business people, accountants, lawyers, people you'd dealt with, and that you send in your education profile. I approached it with a large degree of trepidation. Can I do this? Has my brain been trained the right way? They sent you a lot of stuff to read before you went. An enormous amount of information. I was reading and making notes and thinking, Hell, are they going to ask questions? It was their way of preparing the ground. And I got accepted.

At Harvard applicants were chosen because we had reasonable profiles and businesses of certain sizes. Obviously they knew we'd be able to understand balance sheets and basic business practices. It cost me around US$100,000 and ran during January for three weeks a year, for three years, 1989–91.

We had five very good professors — nearly all of them semi-retired or retired — who had come back to teach because they loved doing this course with the entrepreneurs. They said that they learned more from the entrepreneurs than we ever learned from them.

The basis of the programme was case study work, the same as their famous MBA programme. We did three case studies a day for six days a week for three weeks: very intensive. The facilities alone were marvellous: we had a common room, eating facilities and 12 dorms, all very well put together.

In terms of the attendees, we were very much a mixed group, about 45 per cent foreign or international entrepreneurs and 55 per cent Americans. I got a lot out of the professors but I also got a huge amount out of the other participants because they mixed us up a lot and put us in different study groups. The idea was that you'd study in the evening and then you'd come back in the morning before breakfast and rehash what you'd just read and then appoint a spokesman to represent the group. In the end I thought, You know what — bugger this! I could speed-read so I would read the course material, look at the questions that I could answer and then a group of us would go to the pub and discuss it there. I used to say to them, 'You read that one thoroughly, I'll read this one.' We skimmed the rest. I'm not being facetious, that was just our way of working. I took it very, very seriously: it was a wonderful opportunity.

There were, in all, 110 of us. It really was the highest calibre of participants. There was an Indian billionaire, there was a guy who lived in Switzerland and was an industrialist. (Some years later he died in a light plane crash in Northland; lovely fellow, terribly tragic.) The whole thing was like joining the marines or an arm of the services. You were at boot camp but it was like officer training. It was hugely challenging. You're not supposed to have any contact with your company at all, but I used to get pouches every day; I had to. It meant that on top of everything else I was doing on this comprehensive course, I was reading and answering huge piles of business correspondence. Which involved the inevitable call to the dean's office.

Of course they wanted to make sure they had your attention, your 100 per cent focus. I like to think I'm multi-faceted and I can handle all that stuff, but it was very challenging.

After you did two study sessions in the morning and you went to three lectures, then you broke for lunch and then you had to do some exercise. They had very good facilities and I love my sports. But that was the time I took to go through all my business stuff. Hence a session with the dean.

'We notice you haven't registered for any of the sports.'

'Oh I turn up, sir, and do a bit of exercise.'

He said, 'Owen, the reason we're professors at Harvard is because we've learned a few things about human behaviour along the way . . .'

And I thought, Here we go.

Then he changed tack. 'Now, I remember Wilson Whineray, he came here and he was the one who persuaded me to start the rugby programme. I shared his love of sport and his love of New Zealand so I'm prepared to overlook this if your behaviour changes.'

'Undoubtedly, sir, undoubtedly.'

The problem was after that the instructors at the gym took a keen interest in me; they used to bring me to the front of the callisthenics class, so they could keep an eye on me!

Once we hit our straps, I loved it, absolutely loved it. All the reading, the case studies we did on all sorts of different companies, all they were doing was expanding our thinking. Anything you said could be right or wrong.

The net result was that suddenly my confidence developed. I can remember exchanges. There was one guy, he was a really sharp little fella, a venture capitalist. We were heatedly engaged in an argument about the worth of a certain enterprise. The professor, Salinger was his name, was very good at interacting. I said I thought the figure to offer was $25 million.

And this guy Rick came right back at me, saying, 'I disagree entirely. Anyway, this is what I do for a living and based on this kind of cashflow it's worth 30 million dollars.'

Salinger said, 'Right, right, hold it, and let's get a consensus here. Those who believe Owen is right, raise your hands, those who believe that Rick is right raise your hands.'

Most people believed I was right.

This guy, in absolute frustration, said, 'For f**k's sake, Owen, what's the difference between 25 million and 30 million dollars?'

And I said, 'Five.'

That broke it up.

Even he started to laugh and said, 'Well, you got me there.' We had a chuckle and a beer afterwards.

There was a guy from Tanzania, Girrish, his business owned 38 companies and he was in my dormitory. We were sitting there one Sunday morning reading the papers and someone said to him: 'What are all these companies you own?'

He said, 'We're in petrol distribution, travel, this and that.'

'Well, you must be a pretty important group in Tanzania.'

And he said, 'We *are* Tanzania.'

Then another bloke, who was sitting with *The Wall Street Journal*, said to him, 'Hey Girrish, what do you think your group is worth?'

'Five billion.'

Everyone stopped and looked at him and said, 'You're kidding!'

And he said, 'No, no, five billion. Five billion shillings.'

Someone said, 'Mate, it's 20 Tanzanian shillings to a US dollar.'

He was only about five foot two but he stood up with great aplomb and said, 'Five billion is five billion.'

It was that level of kinetic humour and intelligence that was absolutely astounding.

One day three guys came and they sat at the back of the lecture theatre. They looked like clones, all in their seventies. We didn't know who these people were and they didn't identify themselves.

We were doing this case study on two guys who were partners in a software business. One was an adventurous, entrepreneurial guy, one was a very strong Catholic family man. They were good friends and their families were good friends but they had a different ethos to each other. A third person was their lawyer, also very good friends with them both.

What had happened, a long time back, was the two friends had gone to their lawyer and said, 'Look, we're on the verge of making a decision on whether to go public or not and whether to expand.' One of them was all for it, the other not.

He said, 'Look guys, I've known you two since school, so here's what we'll do. In two weeks, on Friday at 4pm, both of you make a sealed bid for the company and give it to me. And we'll all agree that the higher offer prevails.' So they did this.

Now, the professor was explaining all of this while these guys sat at the back, not saying anything but just smiling.

The professor said that on the given day the envelopes were

opened and the go-getter, adventurer type obviously put the higher bid in. It was about $14 million, from memory. That guy took the company public and made a squillion. The other guy took his proceeds of the sale and did a huge amount of things for the community and his family, and also fulfilled a lifelong desire to climb Mt Everest. We all went 'Wow!' He's got seven children and so many grandchildren when they all meet for Thanksgiving they have to hire a hall.

Then the three guys at the back identified themselves and told the story of what had happened. As a little surprise Harvard put on a cocktail party afterwards so we could mingle with these guys.

We asked them whether they had any regrets and the guy who climbed Everest said, 'Only that I hadn't done it ten years earlier.' He said climbing Everest was a real effort but he did it. The guy who made a squillion donated more than half of it to charities. He's the one that proved you could do it.

Somebody said to the entrepreneur, 'Can you point out one single thing that actually made you so successful?'

'No problem with that at all,' he replied, and he was laughing away. 'I employed the very best consultant I could find . . . my ex-partner here.'

It was one of the most fascinating case studies we did and these were the actual people. It was amazing what you got exposed to.

Harvard can open all the doors. I remember a dinner at the end of one of the three-week sessions in the Kennedy Museum. All the original old masters paintings were taken out of storage and displayed. They must've had 20 security people. Over dinner they played some of the key tapes of the Kennedy era, and video footage as well. There was one in particular I remember, absolutely phenomenal.

It was in the Oval Office. Bobby Kennedy was on the phone, he was Attorney-General.

'Good morning, Governor Wallace, this is Robert Kennedy, Attorney-General, I'm ringing on behalf of the President. Governor, we are very disturbed with this situation in Alabama.' (It was during the time they were blocking the African American students from entering an Alabama University auditorium.) 'The President made a decision that unless you conform to the presidential authority we're going to mobilise the National Guard and move it in.'

Wallace was on speaker and he said, 'Well, that may be all very well but I'm the Governor of this state . . .'

And John Kennedy said, 'Bobby, give me the phone. Wallace, this is John F. Kennedy, President of the United States. I'm giving you a direct order, if you don't follow it I will take steps to remove you from office and move the National Guard in and declare a state of emergency in the state of Alabama. I will close the entire assembly until we bring law and order into your state. Do you understand me, Governor?'

'Yes sir, I understand.'

'Are you going to comply with this presidential order?'

'I'll do it immediately, sir.'

'Thank you very much.'

Breath-catching stuff. One of those moments in history.

They took us to Faneuil Hall, which was the City Hall in Boston where the forefathers had met and really shaped the future of the United States. We had a dinner there, in the banquet hall, and it was spectacular. They brought out all the

ABOVE | Mum (Decima Irene) and Dad (Owen Arthur), circa 1955.

BELOW | The Albertian Hockey Club 1959 tour of Fiji. Back row: G.R. Green (capt.), W. Kettle (vice-capt.), A. Dawson, K. Wagstaff, R.W. Lauder, W.I.C. Saul, T.L. Thomas and E. Burlinson. Middle row: K. Sherson, H. Thomas, M. Gordon, O.G. Glenn and R. Caley. Front row: Mr O.S. Oakley (manager), J. Anslow, B.W. Bull, L. Gutry. Mascot 'Albert'. Games played 7, won 5, lost 2.

ABOVE | Friends' gathering, 1960.

BELOW | My hockey team at Harrods, London, 1961.

ABOVE | Me with my brother Michael, his then-wife Joyce, and Mum and Dad in 1961.

BELOW | Me with Mum and Dad in 1964.

ABOVE | Early stalwarts in DCL. L–R: Michael Sinclair, Bill Brokamp, Bob Davies and me.

BELOW | The office warehouse at DCL. 'Where there's muck, there's brass.'

ABOVE | A proud grandmother. With Angie, Jenny and Sue.

BELOW | Mum and sons, 1999.

ABOVE | With my children Michelle, her boyfriend, Catherine and Chris.

BELOW | With Kerrin McEvoy and horse *Second Coming* who
ran third at the Melbourne Cup, 2000.

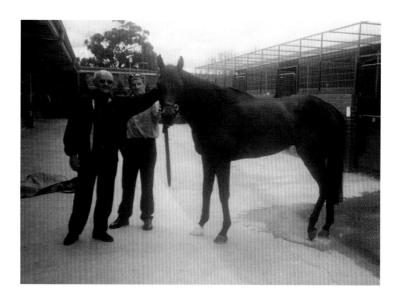

ABOVE | Singing with Howard in Rotorua. L–R: Johnny Anslow, Malcolm Gordon, me and Sir Howard.

BELOW | John Anslow, Malcolm Gordon, me, Jimmy Keir, Gerry Merito and Sir Howard Morrison, 12 December 2003. Gerry Merito was a prominent member of the Howard Morrison Quartet. He wrote 'My Old Man's an All Black', 'The Battle of Waikato' and many others.

ABOVE | With ex-partner Robin Lyon and her son Baydon at Blandford Lodge, Matamata.

BELOW | Back to school, pictured with Baydon.

old banners and they recreated the history. They treated us so well. They opened the inner sanctum.

Unfortunately I didn't really stay connected to all those guys. I was put in charge of the first reunion, which I held in the Virgin Islands. I centred it around a mini Olympics and we had a lot of fun. Over the years people have drifted. Some keep in touch with me, but on an individual basis.

But from a business point of view, it's kind of like the gift that keeps on bringing pleasure. The opportunities you get from being alumni along with being able to ask the university to help with certain things remind you that Harvard is a very powerful institution. Very powerful. Someone told me once, 'They can take your dignity, they can take your assets, but they can never take your education away from you.'

What Harvard taught me was how to broaden my knowledge. Harvard had tonnes of reading material on the subjects that were so relevant to my business. Every time you did a case study, a professor would say, 'Why don't you read this article?' The professors also said that even after we'd gone back to work we should give them a call if we wanted to bounce an idea around. And I did. I'd ring up with a problem and they'd tell me which book to read.

What Harvard really said to me, was, 'Hell, Owen, this is a peek in the window of all the things you haven't had a chance to learn yet.' And so I took a heap out of it.

What Harvard provided me with as well, finally, were mentors. I really hadn't had mentors. When I needed advice I sought it. It was mainly in the areas of either taxation or industry abnormalities — such as the challenges I'd had with Korea and Brazil — those were the occasions when I called on help. I didn't have anybody. My father had died prematurely. There was nobody in my life who I could turn to for advice, till now. I didn't have supportive wives. I used to find when I went on family holidays that I'd feel immense disengagement. My business life was on a different plane. Not that I rejected the idea of being with my family, not that at all.

When we graduated, the class actually wanted to make me the valedictorian to give the final speech, but I said no. There was another guy there, Jess Owen was his name, very intelligent guy. He made an absolutely stunning speech. All that said, it was an extremely proud moment when I got my diploma. I have it hanging on my memorabilia wall in Sydney. It really means something special to me.

And I guess what it means is acceptance. I used to feel that I didn't make the grade because I didn't get to go to university.

Two significant and wonderful things happened to me through the 1990s: in 1992, after the heartache of the divorce and custody battles, Robyn Lyon came into my life. We were together for 10 glorious years, and are still very much close friends, soul mates even. After the troublesome marriages I'd had, it was a blessing to have the companionship of someone so loyal, honest and true.

My views on women, then, have been shaped by the ones that have come through my life. Ultimately, I find women a mystery. Many women that I've met, though, are totally open to change — much more so than men — right throughout their lives. This can be good — they can adapt their minds and behaviour to any given situation — but they can shift their loyalties quickly, too, depending on circumstances. On the other side of the coin, I think that a lot of women, once they lock into a relationship with a man and have children with him, develop a very fixed outlook on what they want from life and this outlook ends up having very little to do with the man they married. It then becomes about status, and not too much else. I believe that women who are successful usually achieve their success without men because they have significant amounts of self-determination, willpower and brains. They don't need us! I suppose that what I finally realised, and it took me a long time, is that it's more important for me to understand a woman than for a woman to ever understand me. I don't regret that: you learn these things as you go along.

Towards the end of the decade, another lady came into my life, the motor yacht *Ubiquitous*. Robyn launched her in Freeport, in the Bahamas, in 1999, a wonderful moment. I have spent more and more time on my boat; I entertain people in her relaxing surroundings, and as much as I ever wind down, I find that even I relax when on board. I have always loved the sea, and the freedom that comes with it. When I left the US in 2003, it was to quite literally leave *terra firma* and spend some time going anywhere for a while, but being based in Monaco.

I have to say, I was very happy when I left the United States. I revoked my right to work, doing so on 31 December 2003 in Nassau, in the Bahamas, aged 63. I had to. The plan was to sell the company. If I'd stayed in the United States and sold the company I would have had to pay a significant capital gains tax.

I told the ambassador in the Bahamas I was going to live in Monaco, and he said: 'Oh, Mr Glenn, it's a lovely place.' Pause. 'Won't you miss America?'

I said, 'Well, I will for many reasons, many, many reasons.' I chatted to him about the quality of the education, the great sporting achievements and the competitive ethic. I continued,

'America is a nation that achieves; America gave me my start in business. I have a lot to thank America for. And gosh, you keep us safe wherever we are, the Kiwis.'

And he said, 'Well, that's nice to know.' And he said, 'Well, I wish you luck.'

One of the things I love about America is that it's probably got a mixture of everything. I mean, will a true American please stand up?! Everyone in the States seems to come from everywhere else; everyone is a wonderful mix of blood and heritage and race: it makes for a fascinating and complex population, and one that, in a sense, makes the idea of being 'all-American' an oxymoron. It truly is a melting pot.

By the time I'd left the US and was based in Monaco, I was travelling so much that I was, in effect, living all over the globe. Monaco was where I 'parked the boat', I suppose. It was during this period that I had two very serious health scares. As a result, I have a very pragmatic view of my own mortality. Thinking of all that reading I did at Harvard and beyond reminds me that one of these near-death events, in a roundabout way, helped with the reading: it clarified my intellect, or at least so the good doctor told me.

I had an operation for an epidural haematoma, during which they took my skull off, cauterised all the membranes in there and literally cleaned my brain. That was in 2008.

Professor Neil Kitchen, who's the best neurosurgeon in the world, said, 'You know, Owen, you will think more clearly now. You will be able to push your brain in directions that you've never even considered before. We did a D&C on your brain.' That means a dilation and curettage, which I would normally consider being a woman's operation (!), but it totally cleaned up my brain. Neil said, 'We pulled it all apart and put it all back together. You will be amazed at the clarity of thought.'

And I was. He was right.

I got a similar message from the heart surgeon who did my quadruple bypass, Alex Stein. He said, 'I have given you back 25 years of your life. How you handle that, Owen, and how you shorten it, is up to you.'

Working backwards (that's what the D&C has done for the clarity of my thinking!), when I had the heart operation, which was in 2001, they gave me a series of medications including beta-blockers, which is pretty standard for someone in that situation. But the doctors made an error. Instead of giving me 10 mg of beta-blockers a day they gave me 100 mg. In the end my pulse actually went down from 90 to 40. I should have died. I should have had a stroke. Instead I was in a restaurant in Long Beach having lunch, and as I got up and walked across the floor I just went . . . boom! And as I fell I hit my head very hard. That caused the ruptures in the membranes of my brain. So I was whisked off to hospital, where I underwent a series of tests and they said, 'No, nothing wrong with him.'

On another occasion I ended up in Malaysia in a hospital where I was told my skull was full of blood. Fair enough. I carried on again. I should have died. I got to Hong Kong and I was going to get back on a plane to London when my friend in Hong Kong said, 'Owen, you don't look well at all.'

So I went into hospital and they drilled two holes to relieve the pressure. Apparently when they drilled, the blood came out like a fountain. I spent three and a half weeks there recuperating and then headed off to Valencia. While I was there I went for another test, same thing. They hadn't cured the problem. Then I had to fly in an air ambulance to England. I had to get special permission to fly at low altitude because of the pressure. Neil Kitchen told me that had I gone on a normal flight my head could have exploded!

I arrived into his hands at the Royal Neurological Hospital in London. When I got to him he took the top of my skull off and then they put a clamp on my head. I could not move for three days. Not my style. They knew that, so I was under constant surveillance. I couldn't even get out of bed, do anything. I couldn't move, every bodily function had to be attended to. I couldn't even scratch. I had to ask the nurses to scratch me. But I couldn't even sleep. Horrendous. I had to be woken every two hours for medication.

They had African male nurses and this guy came in at two in the morning or something.

He woke me up: 'Pills.'

And I said, 'Oh yes, okay.'

I was sort of trying to wake up and he said again, 'Pills.'

I said, 'Okay. I'll take them.' Then he grabbed my jaw. And I'm not a violent person but I whacked him.

And he ran away!

In the morning Neil Kitchen came in and he said, 'I heard you had a little altercation earlier with the night staff.'

And I said, 'Well, here's what happened,' and explained.

'Oh God,' he said, 'you know, I'm sorry. Obviously he was a new recruit.'

And I said, 'Look Neil, I'm paying whatever it takes, there's no question of that. You have looked after me but I tell you what. I'm checking out.'

He said, 'You can't.'

I said, 'I am checking out.'

He asked, 'Why? Because of that?'

And I said, 'No, you haven't got bloody Sky and the All Blacks are playing Wales on Saturday.'

So I rang up the Australian Nursing Association in London and they sent me Aussie nurses to care for me around the clock. They had to be very careful to make sure I didn't fall over. 'Make sure I wake up for the All Blacks game!' I told them. And they did. I was taken very good care of. I recovered very quickly.

Having faced death, I am absolutely at peace with it. So much so, if the good Lord took me now I'd be ready. I'll have to take a chair with me because there'll be some negotiation up there but anyway . . . I honestly don't fear death at all. I just don't want to linger. Just take me.

The heart and epidural were two occasions when He could have just tapped on my shoulder and said, 'Time to go, Owen,' but for some reason He wanted me to hang in and stay so I just got on with it. And I never stopped running the company. When I went in for the heart operation, I was lying on an operating table in Los Angeles and Alex Stein was standing there in full operating kit and I'm saying to my PA at the time, 'Now Lauren, what we have to do, we're going to do this, we're going to set up the Board, and I want so and so to be the acting chairman until I get out of this bloody place.'

And Alex was saying, 'Owen, I am not taking the responsibility if you don't let me operate now, it's that urgent.'

I said, 'Look, I only need another minute.'

'Let us give you a pre-med.' The bugger shot something into me and that was that.

The heart thing started on *Ubiquitous*, off the Isle of Wight. I got this very bad heartburn which was, as I later discovered, really a heart attack. I drove to London, flew to Philadelphia and that was the first time I rolled the dice. We got up to the airport and parked somewhere because I didn't feel well when an Indian minicab driver drove over Lauren's foot. He was yelling and screaming and so I got angry — I keep saying I'm not normally a violent person (!) — and this guy is shouting obscenities at me in Hindi and of course I understand some Hindi and I was not impressed with what he was saying. So I just turned around and in a flash of rage I put a fist right through his windscreen.

And then my hands were dripping blood and he called the cops, and the cops arrested me. They said, 'Well, we're going to have to take you to hospital first and then to the station and we'll have to lock you up for the night.'

And I said, 'Look, I'm flying out and I'm not well. Why don't I just pay for his windscreen?' He said, good old English bobby that he was, 'We can't be a part of that, especially if the minicab driver wants to pursue the charges.'

But he was also pragmatic. 'What we're going to do, my colleague and I, we are going to walk down the terminal, and when we come back, if he doesn't press charges, sir, that's the end of the matter.'

I looked at this bloke, who was about six foot three, and I said, and I have no idea to this day where it came from, 'Do you play rugby for Hounslow?' I suppose because we were in Hounslow, at the airport, although, obviously, he could've been from anywhere. My hand was still dripping blood, by the way.

He said, 'Yeah. How did you know?'

I said, 'Oh I'm a New Zealander, you know, and I watch a lot of games.'

He said, getting a bit more engaged and friendly, 'Yeah, I play lock.'

I said, 'Well, you're hardly going to play halfback!'

'Quite right, sir. You ever meet Colin Meads?'

And I said, 'Yeah, I have actually, I have.'

'*Right-oh* constable, we're just going for a walk now. You won't go anywhere, sir?'

I said, 'No, I'll be right here.'

My PA talked to this Indian guy's boss and we paid £250 for an £80 windscreen. He came back and said he didn't want to press charges any more.

So that was that. I got on the plane . . . probably still, in effect, having a heart attack.

So when I got to Philadelphia — I was staying with people I knew, an Australian woman and her husband, whom I had met in Nassau — and during dinner, this woman's father, who was also there, he looked at me and he said, 'Can I have a chat to you, Owen?'

We went into another room, and he said, 'I need to take you to hospital immediately. You are not well. I'm a doctor. I am actually the head doctor for NASA.' He just happened to be home on leave.

He said, 'I'd advise you to go straight into hospital now.'

I protested. I said, 'I've got to get to LA.'

He said, 'Well, it's your life but . . .'

So I flew to LA and when I got off the plane my daughter Jenny was there and drove me straight around to the hospital: that was it. I was lucky with both the heart attack and the brain rupture. The Good Lord kept me alive. I think He's amused by me. 'Hey Moses, turn the screw a little bit . . .'

They say it comes in threes, and the third thing I had was called a TIA (or transient ischaemic attack, effectively a mini-stroke). This was after the other two scares.

I was having a meeting with a colleague from the Lazard Bank in London in the middle of the day and we sat down to have a cup of coffee at a café off Berkeley Square, and I lost the use of my legs. He sort of carried me into a cab, took me home. We tried to get hold of my surgeon, Neil Kitchen, but he was away. Eventually I got an appointment with another guy, a good guy, too, and he put me through all the tests, MRIs and so on, and they couldn't figure out anything. They were still trying to diagnose it all, and kept me in hospital.

I got up in the middle of the night, swung my legs over, stood up and with help I went for a wee. That was encouraging because I couldn't even walk before. Then when I got up in the morning, before anybody came in the room, I could walk. When the doctor came in at 7am, because he was worried about me, he said, 'How are you feeling?'

I said, 'Well, I think I'm a bit better.' And I stood up and went *cha cha cha!* Did a tap dance.

And he said, 'You bloody fraud.'

Then my PA and executives, etc. came in. They were all worried and I did the same thing for them.

What the doctor said was that I'd had a TIA. A very tiny blood clot went into my brain and cut off the signals to my legs. I'd said to my executive assistant earlier, as soon as it happened, 'Get rid of the lease on the flat in London, get me the Rolls-Royce of wheelchairs, we'll have to put ramps into my Double

Bay property. I'll need nursing help around the clock.' So I gave them all these instructions and they say to this day that they didn't understand how I could do that. Me, I just thought, Oh well, I can't walk, get rid of the sports car I've got and get me a van with the equipment. I rattled it all off.

They said, 'Aren't you worried?'

I said, 'What's there to worry about? I'll probably have to sell the new yacht unless we can put ramps in at the back.'

But then I started walking again, thanks Lord. These things come along to test us.

> *I'm often asked what would have happened if I hadn't sold OTS Logistics (Overseas Transport Services), how I might have seen things unfolding.*

CHAPTER 5 —
THE FINAL SALE AND THE NEXT PURCHASE

'EAGLES DON'T FLOCK.'

I'm often asked what would have happened if I hadn't sold OTS Logistics (Overseas Transport Services), how I might have seen things unfolding, but it's a redundant question. If I'd stayed in the business another 10 years I would have no idea what challenges we would face in this period. I can tell you what challenges are there now and possibly for six months ahead, but I would only have a broad idea of what was to come. However, in my mind I already had blueprints going forward if certain things happened or if certain things didn't happen: the amount of capital required, the management processes and the tax obligations. Business is a work in progress all the time.

One thing I would have done if I'd stayed is that I would have put $100 million in for acquisitions. You grow that kind of company through strategic acquisitions, not so much organic growth. I'd already laid out the 14 companies to buy. I'd already contacted them all.

I said to the incoming investor, 'Here's what you do. And here are the companies you should acquire, and here are the people you should talk to in order to facilitate those acquisitions. And you buy in India, you buy in Germany, you buy in South Africa. I've been to see them all. I've started the ball rolling. All 14 companies will cost about $180 million if *I'm* buying them because they're built on existing relationships.'

I knew a company in a key strategic country, headed by a great guy. So I went and spoke to him. It went like this.

I said, 'How much of your business do we carry?'

'In imports you're carrying about 90 per cent. And our exports: we send you about 78 per cent.'

'So we're actually extremely important to you?'

'Oh yes, obviously.'

'What's the future of your company?'

'Well, I would eventually like to sell.'

I said, 'Who to?'

He said, 'You! How could I go anywhere else? You could start up here and I would lose all my business. That's why I have to sell to you.'

He calls me 'my dear friend'. It's very sweet. Every time I visited him on business, he'd call the family together for dinner and they'd all come as a courtesy. He's got thousands of employees. It's a big company.

But Europe will be the greatest challenge for OTS in the future. Again, acquisitions rather than organic growth. I'm thinking back to when Mainfreight bought Wim Bosman. It wasn't because they were a very good trucking company — Mainfreight are much better — it was because they *gained membership* in Europe. It's what Mainfreight does with that business and how they expand it throughout Europe that counts rather than the profits of the business itself. That's why they bought it. Good move.

You try to do that organically like, say, TNT did: down the tubes. Their thinking was, We can do it, we've done it in Australia. We now dominate Australia, so we'll do the same in Europe. They didn't even get on *the first rung* in Europe. They poured money into it and all in the wrong direction.

Whereas the way I grew Europe was completely by acquisition. A good example is Comfreight. I couldn't even get proper and useful information out of them when we were trying to buy them. I had to make a decision to go over and acquire the company warts and all, and boy did it have warts. In fact at the time of writing they're still battling in arbitration.

The South Africans, the Germans, the Indians, the Chinese, they're all nationalities that I worked with. I set them all up in my company and as my agents. I know which companies I'd buy and it would not just be those which would contribute a better than 10 per cent return. It would be the synergy between what those companies would bring and the rest of the system, which would be more like a 22 per cent return. OTS made $44 million in 2010, probably a little less in 2011. Buying those companies, the ones that would best complement what we already had, could have increased the earnings to about $54–55 million and the turnover to US$1 billion. I put that to the incoming investors.

The price I negotiated for OTS was fair. In my mind it was lock, stock and barrel and the smoking gun. Gone! My mind is already on other things. I can't compete (legally), because of restraint of trade, so I won't; it's not my intention to dishonour my agreement. I'd certainly buy it back at half price in a heartbeat.

Charlie, who is now running OTS, is honest and nice. And all the management in place are capable of carrying out what's required of them, to do the tasks they've been given; but if you want to break through and create a $100 million company from $44 million, you need a different style of management, you need different people, you've got to get into new businesses, you've got to recruit differently.

I'll explain my thinking. If I'm interviewing you to set up a project division for me and your experience is in projects, I have to convince you, or, more correctly, *you have to become convinced*, that what I'm about to offer you is a huge opportunity, better than the one you've currently got. I would have done my homework on you. It's all those bits of information coming together, how you assemble them and how you express them, and if you see the glint in the guy's eye or if he's not looking, if he's gazing around. It's all that stuff. If he looks at his watch, keeps adjusting his collar or whatever. *All* that body language. I sense when you're losing a person and how you get them back. It's just like fishing — what happened? Did he dive low? What happened? Where's this f**king fish?!

So, where the business goes from here will be interesting to see. I won't deny it, it feels very strange not to be involved any more, to be cut off from everyone I used to work with. When you've built a company from absolute zero, it's part of your fabric, it's you. It's like having a limb amputated. But it's not like I'm rolling around in my wheelchair, I've got a bit to keep me going . . .

Which brings me to my latest, most public purchase. It's a well-known fact: I love sport. I loved playing it when I could, I love watching it, and almost any code will do: rugby — union and league, test hockey, cricket and golf. It's just been a constant through my life, a love of sport.

The latest and most obvious example of my sporting involvement is my stake, with Eric Watson, in the New Zealand Warriors rugby league team. Now I'd known Eric by his reputation as a significant thoroughbred owner, and our paths had crossed. We met up again a couple of years back at a dinner at Annabel's in London and I guess you could say I got closer to him, got to know him a bit better. I've always been a rugby union man, but I knew Eric had an interest in the Warriors and

I said, 'Look, I've watched a lot of league, I enjoy the game. Would you ever see me as a shareholder?'

He said, 'Let me think about that.'

Somehow that leaked out into the media, I got questioned about it, then it dampened down a bit. But it came up again, and we talked a bit more. Then, with the first game of the 2012 season being at Eden Park, we rushed a deal through and in about six weeks it was done. And now I do a lot of things with Eric on a whole lot of different fronts, and it's great. I really enjoy the guy. And of course, like me, he's big on the horses — he has about 100, I think, but, and I always tell him this, he doesn't *really* have anything decent to rival mine!

I've been involved with horses seriously for well over a decade now. It came about when I was on my yacht in Auckland, and some friends I was entertaining had brought along some guys who were involved in various syndicates and we got talking. They asked me to get involved, even though I knew nothing about horses, and so, under their advisement, I took 10 per cent in a horse . . . and it came third in the Melbourne Cup! And I thought, This is easy! They let me in on a lot of good horses that performed reasonably well and then I went out to the Karaka Bloodstock Sales, with a partner, Gerard Peterson, who is a very good selector of horseflesh, and we did well. About two years ago I summarised my income and expenditure from horses and I was about $1.6 million up. Mainly due to *Railings* and *Monaco Consul* and *Head Turner*, so . . . I was lucky, obviously. In all, I've had, I think, six runners in the Melbourne Cup. Some people go their whole lives and never get a horse even *entered* in the Melbourne Cup.

Horses, then, were something Eric and I had in common.

We now have some other businesses we've invested in together, and the most notable, or notable in media terms, anyway, is the Warriors.

Why the Warriors? They've done a good job. They've put their stamp on the game. To be in the finals four out of the last six years is no mean feat. I believe Eric and I will take this venture to greater heights, too: we're going to put a lot more of our resources and profits into youth. It lines up perfectly with my Help: Make a Difference programme through the Glenn Family Foundation.

The Glenn Family Foundation have reached an agreement with the Kids Can Foundation, who do an immense amount of good. In 2012 they'll give out 20,000 raincoats. They give children shoes; they provide meals in schools. It's fantastic, because some of these children get nothing. Kids Can impresses me because all their money is privately raised.

I think rugby league is just going to take off in New Zealand. That's going to happen in its own right, but I do believe union is faltering, and you have to point the finger at the administration. Those threats about pulling out of the next Rugby World Cup, made by people who don't speak on behalf of us all, at all. This is our nation's heritage we're dealing with. Interestingly in all my time, no one from the rugby union in New Zealand has ever contacted me for support. Except Gordon Tietjens, and I've done a lot for the Sevens boys, had them on the boat, that kind of thing. But no one else.

For the youngsters, though — and this is where Eric and I want to focus with the Warriors — sport can be a way out. On top of that, I believe that the kids will get through to the adults. Some kid gets selected to a team and he's off to play for the

'Hamilton Hounds' or whoever. I believe even the bullies, the abusive dads, will take pride in that, and maybe it'll make them think, and act, a little differently.

I just like to be involved, to be doing things, making things happen. A good friend said a wonderful thing about me once, 'I compare Owen to an eagle. Eagles don't flock.' I like to lead the way.

I'm *always* on the BlackBerry, it never leaves my side and it's *always* on. I'm never out of touch, ever. I still get messages all the time, just like it was when I was running the business. People may get messages from me at 3am. I'm up late at night or I might be an early riser. It's all the same. Either one.

The closest I get to relaxing is when I'm on *Ubiquitous*, my yacht, and even then I'm in constant touch with business and my philanthropic foundation.

How do I decide where to go next, what to do next? My PA goes with me everywhere but I certainly decide where to put the time in and what I want to do. There's no one central theme to everything. If I want to go and do something, I do it — if I feel like going to church, then I go to church. If I feel like singing and I'm in Kalimpong then I ask the teachers to assemble the children — 'Come on kids' — who love to sing, and we sing. A lot of my life is spent travelling on planes. A lot of my life is spent staying in hotels. A lot of my life is spent watching sport. I never blame anybody else if I'm idle.

Whether I read a report or make a phone call or draft notes about something, I'm always working. My mind is very active and creative. Sometimes I just want to switch off and watch the cricket. Apart from the major health scares, I can say this, I'm never sick. I'm lucky. I never had sick days at school and I can't remember how long it's been since I took a day off sick — 20–25 years? I'm not answerable to anybody so what's a sick day? I work seven days a week. The only time I remember taking off was for my heart operation and my brain operation, but I was under anaesthetic so I've got a good excuse.

I've never smoked in my life — ever. I haven't had a puff. My father died of lung cancer and its complications. I've never taken any drugs ever. I like a beer, I like wine more than beer now and I drink spirits rarely. I have a drink, but not every day, particularly at the moment, on the orders of Dr Ali, my great well-being doctor.

I read copiously, always have, and not just the reports that came through from the business. Normally I'm reading three books at a time, say, a biography, a thriller, a book on health . . . recently I was reading a book of speeches, fascinating speeches. I get a lot of mental stimulation from things like that.

My friend who is a lawyer in Sydney said, 'Owen, I'm going to send you the speech Steve Jobs gave to Stamford University in 2005.' This was when I had just sold OTS. And he said, 'I think it's highly pertinent in your business circumstances.'

I found it fascinating. Jobs gave the students three aspects of his life to consider and think about — that he'd dealt with the cancer, built a business, and been fired by his own company, Apple. I related to the latter — not that I was fired, but that feeling of being ostracised — and to how he worked his way back and got back in. His work ethic was admirable: to think he built up the biggest company in the world on market capitalisation. Apple, bigger than GM, bigger than BHP. It's quite amazing. And he could always see ahead. We lost a genius when he died, an absolute genius.

My point is, which is why I read so many biographies, we can learn a lot from others. I made up for a lack of formal education to a large extent by reading as much as I could.

A fair question that gets put to me a bit these days is, would I have done anything differently? I honestly don't know how I would've turned out or whether I'd have taken the risks that I took if I had more knowledge. I never followed the rules but I would've hesitated a lot more. I was batting without pads.

Which brings me back full circle to my remaining time and why I'm going to devote so much of it to trying to change things for the better in New Zealand, the country I love.

When I was in India it was during a period after war and there was violence. When independence came to India every British subject had to prove they had at least a grandparent of British origin, which my family did. It was probably the most talked-about circumstance at that time. Unless you had a British passport or British citizenship, you'd be Indian. Cut and dried. The Indians had decided that they didn't want to be a British colony. So the British simply said, 'We're leaving, we just need to establish whether you belong to us or whether you stay where you are.'

Personally, I didn't feel that I belonged. We all felt we were on borrowed time in India. My father had progressed well and had a good job and he was also offered secretary of the Turf Club, which was a big appointment. But he knew he had to leave India; there was no future for us there. He had a look down here, we stayed for three months when I was eight, we went back to India and he said, 'I like New Zealand,' and away we went in 1951.

He was a very smart man, as I've said. It's the little things that make a difference, though. For instance, he never qualified as an accountant so he couldn't get an accountant's salary; he was always paid as an accounts clerk. He had some savings and he bought a house. At that time you could make a decision to apply for New Zealand citizenship when you came of age and, by the time I was 21, I decided to do that. I relinquished my British passport. I went and applied and became a New Zealand citizen and got a New Zealand passport. I finally felt I belonged. I chose a country and I belonged.

The final piece of that puzzle, really, was getting the doctorate. I only got as far as Form Five at school and yet I received an honorary Doctor of Law from the University of Auckland in 2012: yes, that did make me proud. The ceremony was wonderful. I received my doctorate at the same time as Hugh Fletcher. You couldn't get two more different backgrounds. As I said in my acceptance speech, and it was quoted in the *New Zealand Herald*, 'You either give university a go or you build a business school and they'll give you a doctorate.' That was just teasing a bit.

Following that I said, 'I don't take this lightly.' And I don't. That is true recognition and from a number of people whom I greatly respect, too. Before they award the degree they go out to the faculty, I believe, and they ask for comments. I helped the environment, supporting the Leigh Marine Laboratories at Goat Island, and the medical school and the business school, so the comments that came back were totally supportive. There wasn't one dissenting voice: it was a unanimous vote by the council, I was told. That's nice. That just shows that they truly appreciate it. Any time they ask me to do anything, I do it if

I can. They said to me once, 'That factor, that you're readily available to everybody at all levels, carries a huge amount of weight with the student body.'

I love spending time at the university. Staff and students greet me in the halls and it's nice. It's like coming home when I go there; they're just lovely people to know. I've had dinner in their homes and been to lunch at their homes. They come and have a beer with me sometimes. I can ask for help, too. And I found that once you get the University of Auckland stamp of approval on something, like a report, it carries a huge amount of weight. Huge.

I have to ask myself, then, looking back at all this: Where is Owen Glenn going to end up? Let's say I've got 10 years left. What do I want to do in those 10 years? The yacht's a distraction, but I don't stop thinking because I'm on the yacht. I share these experiences with people, take them into a nice environment on the yacht and enjoy their company for a couple of nights and enjoy a couple of dinners. Go for walks on Waiheke. That's my leisure time. I love the sea. I love everything about it.

I get a huge kick out of watching the New Zealand men's and women's teams playing hockey — I donated $1 million to support the Hockey Foundation, and I'm delighted to be able to provide that support. It's their intensity that I love, their desire to win. I see it more in other people than it in myself. I love seeing people challenge themselves. I'm willing to back them. I love it when they say: 'I can do this.' I watch them play and challenge them.

I said to one of the senior men, 'I see you've got all that natural athletic skill, but when you get into the circle you lack the killer instinct. You've got to lay your life on the line. Your sole dedication is to get that yellow ball into the back of that net and anything that stands in your way, take it out.'

This guy said, 'Right.'

I said, 'I want to see mongrel, pure mongrel short of biting the bloke.'

He smiled and said, 'Okay, Owen.'

So, yes, I would've loved to be a sports coach. I would never have said the obvious! But that sporting environment, that feeling of camaraderie, that development of a group of friends of any age, any background, any ethnicity: there's a great satisfaction in taking that forward game by game. I'm a team captain, I'm a team coach-type guy.

Myself, I was an average sportsman but I enjoyed sport and I have been privileged to play with good sportsmen, Olympic hockey players. I wasn't up to their standard but I enjoyed it and I played to my capacity. I remember all the highlights. (I tend to forget all the lowlights!) I played hockey for 20 years and I loved it. I played it because I enjoyed it. Occasionally I did something miraculous. Thankfully I always played with good people, who patted you on the back afterwards and said, 'Well done, that was great.' You enjoyed a beer with them, you enjoyed a cup of tea with them. It was the fellowship that attracted me. I'm very much a people person, in business, sport, philanthropy, everything, really. Interaction.

People talk all the time about money, and even though I am constantly referred to as a billionaire I actually never have been one. It's only quite recently that I could even put $50 million together. Does it give you security? I worked so hard to get security for my young family in the beginning that, yes, it's a good feeling when you can maybe breathe a little bit. I would say that once I had $5 million behind me I felt a little comfortable, in spite of going through a couple of rocky marriages. It took a long time to get over those.

Then, after some time, I had the boat. I bought the villa in Fiji which was Fiji $4 million, bought half the Blandford Lodge farm, and also acquired a home in Double Bay in Sydney. People are calling me a billionaire; it isn't true and I never said that.

With all the public speaking I do, I've been asked, 'Don't you get apprehensive getting up to talk?' I never get apprehensive. I wouldn't have felt that way since quite an early age, in my twenties, maybe. I got better at it with practice. I have an agile mind so I think, Okay, what do they want to hear? Who am I going to appeal to? What progression of ideas am I going to put forward? It never really worried me and still doesn't.

In terms of recognition, the honorary doctorate, as I say, meant a great deal. Being named Entrepreneur of the Year in the US, that was pretty special too. It was in the Century Plaza Hotel in LA (the same place that poor old Bobby Kennedy was assassinated) and the ballroom floor held 3000 people. It was a great surprise; it felt like the Oscars.

I've been given ratu (chief) and ren lapum (master and creator of the Lepcha tribe) status in Fiji and India respectively. When I visit Kalimpong in India, it's like they all know me, which is very sweet, very humbling. I call them 'my children'. These titles are gratifying because they confer respect and they say these people trust me. I've always said that being able to gain people's trust, having integrity, is the most important thing you can achieve and maintain.

It's no secret, particularly in this country, and Australia, too, that people are constantly trying to cut you down. Who are you or who do you think you are? I ignore it. When they get nasty and personal, and a lot of that happens, particularly in the media, I never answer any of that, ever. It's a waste of energy that I can put to better use.

And that's what I intend to do. I intend to make a significant difference in New Zealand's future. Significant. Apart from and beyond my wanting to address the domestic violence we have in our society, I intend to do further work with the university and I intend to work with sports, I intend to make a difference in a lot of New Zealanders' lives. I have no ulterior motive whatsoever that I can think of. I don't even care if they don't want to give me the credit for it. It doesn't worry me. I just think it needs to be done.

I trust that doesn't give the impression that I feel under-appreciated, because I don't. That is not the word. I don't feel understood, perhaps; or not fully understood, anyway. I find that people often treat me with suspicion yet I am very open with my views and what I've done with my life.

I come up with these ideas of how we can all change things for the better, and that implies criticisms unfortunately, because, in a sense they are. But I don't mean to criticise. I often say, 'The government did this right' or 'This is a good move'.

Even with the political parties, I donated to both left and right. I always did. I'm egalitarian and pragmatic. I don't care what political stripe they are; if they're going to do a good job I've been keen to support them.

People will believe what they believe, I suppose. One thing that I hope becomes clear through the telling of my story is that I didn't have it easy. I wasn't handed any of this. Even when I first saw the opportunity with seafreight, when I was in Australia in the early 1970s, it was only that: a vision. A vision without substance. It was a vision I had that I could do a lot better than this, there had to be something better out there. I had to take the risk. And throughout my life I kept taking those chances and increasing my family as I went along. I always grabbed at opportunities.

Maybe it's because my father settled for indifference. My mother was the go-getter. My mother never had the education. She left school when she was 16 and didn't have any support. My dad was the mental giant and a very clever man, but he hid his light under a bushel. I didn't want to end up like my mum and dad. I knew there was something better than that. It wasn't their fault: it was the time, their circumstances. I always thought, Whatever my circumstances I've got to go after something better. Always.

But it took a long time to get there. I probably didn't really feel that I was in command of my life until the mid-1980s, when I sold out to the Sagawa Group in Japan and then bought the company back, because that gave me enough money to have some disposable income and I could buy a decent house. I was pretty quick to say, 'Let's cash in.' I nearly did twice. I did once with the Japanese and I nearly did it again with another deal, but I hung on instead. As I hung on I increased my income.

But I knew at the time, in 2011, having two close brushes with death, that if I died before I sold it, the company would be worth a lot less. I also felt that it was time to do other things.

"

To be a very good salesman you have to be an extremely good listener. It's not what you say, it's what you hear.

"

CHAPTER 6 —
MY BUSINESS PHILOSOPHY

WE CAN'T HAVE EVERYBODY CHARGING AROUND LIKE CAPTAIN MARVEL . . .

I calculated it all once and realised I'd made well over 28,000 sales calls in my business time — all over the world, everywhere from Beijing, Cape Town, Adelaide, Oslo.

Whenever I arrived in a new country, I'd smile when

they'd invariably say to me, 'Well, Mr Glenn, it's different here, you know.'

I've always thought, *What's* different? People are people, psychology is psychology.

What I believe is that to be a very good salesman you have to be an extremely good listener. It's not what you say, it's what you hear. I helped devise a sales course that was the cornerstone of my success. I held the course 28 times, I delivered it, I knew it backwards, it's part of my life.

It was actually based on one delivered by Emery Air Freight who were, in a way, the company that taught me everything in the beginning. Theirs was a five-day intensive course; you grasped the essentials and then you went out with a trainer for two days' active selling. You made actual appointments, went right through the process and the trainer just sat there, observing, I suppose. And it was on one of those calls I discovered I had something beyond just a natural selling ability, a natural calling.

It was the first call I made. It was on the sixth day of the course, on a Monday morning in Sydney, to Twentieth Century Fox. I was sweating because I had to remember all the stages of what I had to say and do.

Near the end of the call I said, 'Mr Jones, if you become convinced that using Emery Air Freight would really improve your service and you can meet your deadlines, who would you have to call to implement your decision?'

And the client said, 'Well, it's Johnny Roxborough in Hollywood, he's in charge of the procurement.'

I said, 'Are you convinced?'

'I'm definitely convinced.'

'Would you mind ringing Mr Roxborough now?'

'Not at all.'

I thought, What the hell have I got here?!

The trainer looked at me and said, 'I don't believe you just did that.'

That was when I realised that I had a real gift for sales.

It's not so much a matter, as some would have it, that you do your bit, you do your best, and then the decision is ultimately up to the client and, hey, if you've done it right, they'll buy. Not at all. For me, I know what the outcome is going to be because, if you look carefully at what I did, there is a crucial point, a pivotal moment. In fact, this is the critical sentence in the whole course: 'Are *you* convinced', not 'if *I* convince *you*'. I've never heard 'no' to that.

And you do not say anything else until he answers. It doesn't matter if the silence lasts for a minute. You can repeat it, 'Shall I repeat that question, sir?'

'No, no, I understand what you're saying, just let me think about it. Okay, I am convinced . . .' You can see the turmoil; you've got them on the hook.

I was 26 when I did that course. I went ahead in leaps and bounds as a salesperson at Emery. It honed my skills, it gave me confidence; it changed my life.

I set my own standards. Always. I always wanted to be the best for myself. If I happened to be in competition with others, they were just there.

That said, to be honest, I never started off with a business philosophy. I simply saw an opportunity after TEAL and Emery. Emery taught me a lot. They were, in my opinion, the best freight forwarder at the time. John Emery senior, who started the company, was a World War II naval commander: he'd been in charge of a substantial part of the US Navy's procurement and supply, and had the opportunity to start his company after the war. They were the first freight forwarder to receive a carrier certificate from the United States Government; he had some very good thoughts on how to run a company, how to measure things. He was very thorough and an absolute whizz on human relations. While I met him only once, the way he ran his business had a significant impact on me.

It's interesting to mention here that whole father-and-son business idea. While I was so impressed with John Emery senior, I met his son (John Emery junior) and he simply wasn't a chip off the old block. The old man was something very special.

For me, he even outdid J.W. Marriott who, of course, prided themselves also on this father-and-son relationship philosophy. J. Willard Marriott, the guy who started the hotel company, had this thing, like a tagline, really, which was: 'If you've got a problem, ring me.' Staying in a Marriott in Torrance, California, in 1993, I had the opportunity to put this claim to the test. I had no hot water in my room. I couldn't get anywhere with the management and so, as the tagline suggested I should, I rang him. I got through to his private secretary and I said, 'Ring him.'

She said, 'I'm afraid he's busy now.'

And I said, 'Can someone call me back?'

'One moment please . . . J.W. Marriott here.'

'Ah Mr Marriott, look, I'm in Torrance, here's the problem . . .'

'And you're on the top floor, are you?'

'Yeah, I'm in the suite, so I'm the first one to run out of hot water.'

'Let me come back to you.'

Next thing the general manager, the assistant general manager, and eight other people came up to my room.

'We'll move you, sir.'

The guy told me that when they designed the building, they didn't put in an adequate holding tank for the hot water.

And I said to him, 'But you've been open three years.'

He told me they'd been having an argument with the builder, and so forth. I told him that they simply couldn't do that to people.

He said, 'No, you're quite right, sir. Under Mr Marriott's instructions, you are not to be charged for your stay with us. We apologise.'

Then everything arrived, fruit, wine, the whole bit. That's all fine, but what I wanted was hot water.

It taught *me* something.

I employed the same philosophy, that idea of being as available as possible to the clients. And as my company grew there was a phase and a period there when I thought I was getting too aloof from the company. I was so busy opening up and buying companies. So we put a survey out to our clients asking them to 'Tell us what we're doing right and then tell us what we're doing wrong'. A lot of criticism came back. I was very surprised, and I realised that I was out of touch with my company. So I put that right. I did a number of things, but one of the first things I did was put in a hotline through to me. Of course every bugger rang! And the trouble with international business is that someone who wanted to talk to me could be anywhere in the world, so I got calls at all times of the day and night.

But it was a very positive step. Even the biggest companies

said they were very impressed. The comment I remember was from one of our biggest supporters, who said, 'Owen, I wouldn't ring you in the middle of the night but the two or three times I've had to make a complaint or had a problem, you've dealt with it.'

I later filtered it back down to my regional managers, although I still had my name on it and said to certain clients, 'Call me if you get no satisfaction.' They called me less and less as they dealt with other people. But it taught me something. What I also did was encourage my people to ring the customers and ask if anyone in the business had given them really exceptional service, and then we mentioned them in our monthly newsletter. That human relations aspect — both internal and external — was very important in the company.

These little things sometimes make a difference but they were all things I had to teach myself. I taught myself most of the aspects of running a business because I didn't have time to study. When I went to Harvard Business School it was like the pieces of the jigsaw finally came together and I could see the picture. I got taught internal controls, human relations, cashflow management. Collect my receivables quicker, pay my payables a bit slower: that's what I learned. I got all of that. But I learned something else critical, too.

The professor, Marty Marshall (officially Harvard Business School Professor Emeritus Martin V. Marshall), said to all of us, 'Now, you're going to go back after this course and create havoc in your company. You'll want to change everything at once. Take my advice: don't do anything.'

He was so right: wait until the third bounce. So that's exactly what I did; I waited. I stood back, watched it all differently with new eyes. I talked to people in the business. I'd ask them what they thought of certain things. Watched. Waited. Observed. *Listened*. That's what I learned from Harvard. And that was worth every cent.

I'd certainly say without question that one of the things that drove me was not wanting to end up in a position of penury or starvation. And as I said in my speech when I received my honorary doctorate, clearly I've survived the first because I've sold my company for nearly half a billion dollars and I look all right for the second! I'm not starving.

While I did the normal things like raising children and paying bills, through all that was a desire that was more than just a desire to succeed. I simply didn't see anything standing in front of me that caused me any concern, and if anything did come up — like the 50 Mile Rule (discussed in Chapter 3) or perceived threats to the business — I just rolled my sleeves up and got stuck into it. My attitude was: How *dare* they stop me? I had all sorts of threats but my attitude always was, Give it your best shot. All that external stuff never worried me.

If some sort of threat or potential hazard to the operation came up, I'd just go back to my thoughts and ask myself: Am I doing the right thing? And if I feel I'm doing the right thing, that's probably the best argument I've got for taking the next action. It's my call.

That's how I liked it. I never had a board of directors because I always own 100 per cent. I had an executive committee which, at its peak, had 13 members. I used to say to them, 'You've all got a say, you've all got a vote but never forget I've got 14 votes.' Of course I would listen to them but ultimately they would say, 'Owen, it's your company.'

If anyone challenges that or suggests it's unusual to not have a board of directors, I simply look at the evidence. I turned $2000 into $600 million, therefore I would say that I made more right decisions than wrong.

My view is that a board of directors would have interfered. Freight is very much a detail business, there's much you have to absorb and know. I would've read millions of words and spoken to thousands of people, not just customers but people all over the world. Shipping companies, lawyers, I was up on Capitol Hill many times in Washington, dealing with the FMC, the various regulatory bodies. How can a board of directors compete with that sort of personal, hands-on experience?

One of the obvious examples of my way of doing business was that no matter where in the world I went and opened up, no matter how much money was at stake, no matter who I dealt with, I always maintained utmost integrity. I never, ever took a bribe or paid a bribe to anybody. Ever. Even in places where it was considered standard practice. Whatever was offered, I never ever took it and I never authorised for anyone else to either.

I question, sometimes, whether my way of operating could even be called a philosophy as such: for me, it was just who I was, who I am, the way I operate. That said, if someone came to me and asked me for my five basic business philosophies, it would come down to something like this:

Number one is passion; you've got to have a passion for whatever you want to do. Even if you're a humble postman. Look at this characteristic in the broadest human sense: not everybody is cut out to be a success in business; we can't have everybody charging around like Captain Marvel, it's just not going to work. But whatever you do in life, in your inner self you must be committed to it. And if you're going to be successful, become passionate about it, whatever it is. If you want to be a postman be the best bloody postman you can be. Go and figure out how to subdue dogs! Whatever it is you have to do, whatever it takes to be the best postman.

When you get up in the morning and you look in the mirror, that reflection looking back at you has to excite you, has to make you feel you're going to do something worthy, and not just for the day: know that you're going to continue to do something worthy and you've got a plan. So passion is the one thing that is the essential ingredient.

Number two is your work ethic. First, take a look at yourself: have you got it? Second, are you willing to employ it to whatever lengths are necessary to make you successful? I believe a work ethic is something that you're born with; I don't think it's something you acquire. It's in you or it's not in you. That work ethic is essential.

Number three is integrity and everything that goes with that — trust, honesty, accountability. Not just in business, but in your personal life as well. Your handshake has to have the same worth as your word. My father taught me that. He said, 'Son, if you shake somebody's hand, it's very important that you look them in the eye and say, "You have my word."' And that has to count. Never mind bits of paper and lawyers and court: if your personal integrity is ever questioned and you don't measure up to it, you're not worthy of doing what you're doing. That was always at the forefront of my mind. When I offered my hand and shook on it, it could be trusted completely.

I just had a case in the sale of OTS, where they started to try to monkey around with the prices. So I wrote to the chairman of the investing company: 'We had a handshake agreement and you said to me that you believed and your grandfather believed that the handshake was the mark of the man. In this transaction, which is now bouncing around the walls, what happened to integrity? I look forward to your answer.' That's all I said to him.

He wrote me back a very nice note. He'd immediately got himself involved back in the deal, because he'd become aloof from it, and he simply said, 'We made a deal, let's stick to it.'

There was some adjustment to the price, and reasonably so, so I met him — maybe not halfway, but a lot of the way there. But this number three, which I think is very, very important, it applies throughout life; it applies when you're buying a house, it applies when you play sport, it applies dealing with your common man or woman: integrity. People assess you from your actions. Not your intentions.

Number four is be magnanimous with your successes and be gracious in your defeats. All is not lost ever; there is *always* a path to recovery if you're down. When you're up it's important to be chivalrous to your opponents or your adversaries. If someone's gone down, lend them your shoulder, just understand their despair, give them some dignity, some face: because they will always remember that.

What happens in international business is that people form opinions, a consensus develops, and a momentum develops.

I've heard said of other people, 'Oh he's okay, he's a good guy, you can take his word for it.' I think that's what enables a person to rise with the cake and say: 'You can work with him,' or 'His word's his bond.' Critical.

Is there a number five? If you can absorb all that and practise all that then the fifth thing has to be something that perhaps doesn't have that much to do with business but has a lot to do with life, and that is: really, *really* do something meaningful to help those who can't help themselves. Whatever the reasons for a person being where they are in life — abuse, or just general circumstances, it doesn't matter — if you can, help them.

Your life has to round up, that's the last page, the personal side. Someone called it squaring the circle. That'd have Pythagoras squirming in his grave, but that's what it is: make a difference.

I'll finish the chapter with a favourite anecdote. People talk a lot about bribery and corruption. OTS was in the process, when I sold it, of pushing a rail link from the American Midwest through into Mexico. Now *that* is a breeding ground of underhand dealings. Being involved in it reminded me of a great anecdote that I heard delivered by Peter Ustinov — he was such a good raconteur that Harvard used to film his speeches, and we saw a lot of them when I was on the entrepreneurs' course. He tells this story, which I think is very informative.

It involved a Mexican called, as you'd expect, Pedro, along with Al, a border security guy. Pedro would cross the border into the United States with a wheelbarrow filled with sand. Later in the day Pedro would walk back into Mexico just on his own. Intrigued, Al started searching the sand, trying to work out what Pedro was smuggling. He'd go through it, dump it, do everything he could with that sand but he never found anything in it. Years later, when they'd both retired, Al was in a bar and Pedro walked in.

And Al said to Pedro, 'You know, you had me stumped. I never quite figured it out. You must have been smuggling something but I just couldn't work out what it was.'

Pedro said, 'Yes, I was.'

Al, dying with impatience here, said, 'So, what was it?'

Pedro says, smooth as silk, 'Wheelbarrows.'

"

What it is you're building is a series of pyramids which leads to the big pyramid. You may have one or two that are a bit shaky but you look at all that as you go along.

"

CHAPTER 7 —
'DARE MIGHTY THINGS'

I'M A CONDUCTOR OF AN ORCHESTRA, AND MY ORCHESTRA IS SCATTERED ALL OVER THE WORLD. MY JOB IS TO GET THEM ALL TO PLAY THE SAME TUNE, IN TUNE.

My father was a man of few words, but they were always important words, worth listening to. One of the things he said which I always remembered was: 'You do what you think is right. Let other people worry about their conscience.'

People are entitled to their opinion, but I'm going to go ahead and do what's right. That's how I've always operated. That's always stuck in my mind. While, like anyone, I'll try persuasion to a certain extent, if I think what I have in mind is right I'll do it, and then I'll sit back and watch the others. Not everyone does the right thing back; that's another lesson I've learned through experience. I've also learned not to take that personally, to cope with that and not take it as rejection.

If people do what I consider to be the wrong thing by me, I get over it pretty quickly. I never, ever hold grudges. What's the point? There are a few people who, over the years, have not acted in my best interests. That's always going to happen when you consider the number of people I've dealt with and the things I have done. I've made a point of simply focusing on remembering the good times. It works well for me.

Despite the massive scale of the business, I'd always managed to engender loyalty from within. Obviously you're not going to have everyone on side, but I think I did really well at maintaining that personal touch, I suppose what people call the 'common touch', for want of a better phrase. When I was in the final stages of selling the company I was amazed at the number of goodwill emails I got, staff wishing me well and thanking me. Maybe I'm still naïve, maybe I just never expect gratitude and so am doubly rewarded when it happens, but it was deeply gratifying. It's times like those when you realise that maybe you made a difference in people's lives, somehow.

One email I got was from a payables clerk, someone I had really no contact with and could barely place, and she wrote, 'You don't know me, Mr Glenn, but I sit at the third desk as you come in the back door, and I just wanted to say . . .'

Totally unexpected. I should've taken more notice of her! I sent her a bunch of flowers, acknowledging her email.

However, I was also amazed at those who didn't bother sending a word, guys who I'd worked with and brought through over 10–20 years, guys earning significant six-figure salaries, who couldn't pick up the phone or send an email. I'm not bitter about it, but just think it's appalling manners, and manners are very important to me. I guess it means that despite all the experiences I've had, I can still be completely surprised by human nature, both good and bad.

It got me thinking about how I built — and sustained — loyalty from my people. Two words come to mind: effective communication — and that's at all levels. Not making speeches from the mountain but absolutely communicating. And again, making sure it's not about good intentions but about good actions. I'd pop in on staff when they were having their sandwiches in the kitchen and ask, 'How have we done today?'

I put in things, earlier on in the piece, such as every time someone made a brand-new booking they could press two buttons on the phone and a bell would ring. What was great was that when you heard that bell ring, everyone would go: 'Yeah!' It's about celebrating success. I'll be honest, the bell-ringing episodes were few and far between in the beginning but as we developed momentum the bloody bell's been going ever since! Staff got a great kick out of that.

I always believe, and always believed, that there should be a reward system, and that, whatever measures you put in, positive reinforcement is delivered by what you say to people, backed up by action. So if somebody made 10 bookings they were acknowledged for having achieved that level of success, and they'd get a voucher for two to take their loved one to dinner. I was very particular about putting in those measures. It's also important that those initiatives are done consistently: you have to reward in good times and bad.

Even in the depths of despair, when things business-wise were very, very difficult, we still had our baseball team and we also had a big picnic day. Everybody would come, from throughout the organisation, and even though the company was as strapped as it was, we would always throw in a couple of hundred dollars for hotdogs and stuff. What it meant was that the staff knew we cared. More importantly, they knew *I* cared, because I would talk to them and ask them about their work, what they thought of the company, how they were going, and what was happening at home.

A step back from that is getting the right people in the first place, and there are a number of ways of doing that.

Whenever we opened in a new country, and we were looking at applicants for the post of country manager, we'd do that in a number of ways: word of mouth, references, advertising, or sometimes we'd transfer one of our own people for a period. But it's critical that you make the best start you can, and you do that by picking the right person. We exercised what is really simply a question of judgement. I'll admit, obviously, that we had occasions — not many — when we didn't pick the right person, but you can normally recognise that you've got the wrong person no later than five and as early as three months into their tenure. And you change that.

Our contracts always had a clause covering an initial period where we could quickly dismiss people without any payouts and redundancy payments and so on. There's the expression they use in the criminal justice system, a probation period, and that's what we called it: they're in and then, if it doesn't work, they're quickly out. That's how you find the right person or transfer the right person in.

Once you had the right person, you'd then instil in them the culture of the company, what you're on about and who you are and what systems you have. It's huge. Everything from the personnel manual to the IT systems to the marketing philosophies, these are all pieces of the jigsaw that they have to understand, absorb, agree to. The minute-to-minute, day-to-day management of how they should run the company based on their location. If you've got the right person — and more or less I've ended up with the right people in all locations — you then build. What it is you're building is a series of pyramids which leads to the big pyramid. You may have one or two that are a bit shaky but you look at all that as you go along.

A good example is South America. We sent a guy down, he was ex-Thunderbird School of Global Management in Arizona, an American who spoke fluent Spanish, lived in Buenos Aires. He opened up for the company in Brazil, Chile, Colombia, Mexico, Costa Rica; there was an acquisition planned for Peru. It had become a very profitable region, making something in the vicinity of US$12 million a year in those countries with the potential to turn that into $20 million in a three- to four-year period. There was a lot of upfront growth ahead of it all.

Capital employed? Less than $2 million. That's a very healthy return. And there's now great infrastructure in all those countries. And this guy had employed, in turn, many Spanish, Brazilian, Portuguese-speaking people, but they all had to have a command of English. He went through the checklist. We instilled in him all our own philosophies and understandings of how we wanted the company run, and he passed it on.

The way I used to put it was: 'I'm a conductor of an orchestra, and my orchestra is scattered all over the world. My job is to get them all to play the same tune, in tune.' That's exactly what I did.

It is, though, one thing, to have certain principles and ways of doing business that you want to instil in your company, but conveying those right down the line is always going to be difficult. Keeping that orchestra in harmony, to continue the analogy. And I did it by spending time with people at all levels. It's no use just talking to the managers.

You take the manager by the hand and say, 'Come with me,' and you go and find a staff member you don't know:

'Excuse me, how long have you worked with us?'

'Well, I started in June.'

'Oh. And did you come straight out of university to us?'

'Yes, I did.'

'What do you think of this industry?'

'Well, it's very exciting. I like working in this industry because something changes every day or every hour.'

'And how do you get on with everybody? Do they treat you nicely?'

And they're all listening in.

And that staff member will say, 'Oh they're very nice and if

I have problems they're all willing to help.'

And so the manager was learning: you're asking and you're listening.

But the crucial thing is I didn't just approach staff by myself: there's no point in that. I took the *manager* and he got the hang of that and he passed it on and all the others would say, 'I think he really cares about us.' And I did.

I always used to say, 'Look, after work I know you guys go down to the Holiday Inn,' or whatever it was. 'I'm going to host a few drinks for an hour, you're all welcome to come, not just the managers.'

And someone would say, 'Oh I wish I had known, I'd have arranged a babysitter,' and so I learned from that. I thought, next time I'll tell her. And because I showed an interest in that very detailed way, they'd all come for drinks, they all felt they belonged, that I was interested in them and their lives. And I was.

The trouble was as the company grew I couldn't be every-where at once. (Ubiquitous!) So I tried to instil this absolutely critical aspect of communicating through all my managers, down through the ranks and, of course, human nature being what it is, some were good at it and some weren't, and some were horribly imperious. It's interesting, though, because the way I'd find out that these poorer-performing managers weren't making the grade was by what was actually happening underneath them. They'd lose touch with their own people, who started moving on in droves; it was then that you could clearly see where the problem lay.

I made it my business as much as I could to talk to people who had resigned or left and I'd ask them, 'Just tell me what we could have done better to keep you as a loyal employee?' And there'd always be something.

They'd come back with: 'Well this is something that stuck in my craw' and 'I was overlooked here' or 'I was supposed to have a review and that was deferred for a month and then another month and it never happened'.

There were always reasons, and I always listened. I followed up on people, even after they'd left, to get an understanding of what had happened and to maybe leave them with a better impression than what they left with. What was surprising was that when they got that contact, some of them actually came back to work for us. All I'd say to them was, 'Look, we've learned from your experience, thank you for talking to me, because it will help us to deal better with the colleagues that you left behind.' That got them.

But if that sounds cynical, it wasn't: I truly meant what I said, I meant it from the heart. I needed to keep humble; I needed to keep listening. So I learned to never, ever shut the door.

From that, one of the greatest measures of our success was that our competitors worked fiercely to recruit our people.

So somebody would say, 'I'm leaving to join Company X.'

I'd respond, 'Well, okay, entirely up to you.' But I'd also say, 'Think for a minute about why they came after you and the eight years that you've put into us. Have you learned anything from it?'

'Oh yeah, I love what I'm doing here but they've made me this offer.' That was invariably what would come back.

I'd say, because often they couldn't really see past that offer, 'What are you *really* doing? Think carefully about that.

All right, they're going to inflate your salary for a while but if you don't give them a pound of flesh, will their management understand your concerns?'

That always made them think. It made them value the support we gave them — above and beyond a good salary and the usual perks — and made them think a bit longer term, with a broader perspective.

Very recently I had news that a long-standing employee, Sandra, died of cancer. She was a lovely, lovely woman and it was very, very sad. But I will look after her family and personal concerns, privately. The question I am always asked: why do you do all this? All this 'extra mile' stuff? And I suppose the answer is that I'm going to have to ask my mum and dad! What did they instil in me?

I also learned a great deal from John Emery senior, particularly how to value every single employee. Certainly Emery Air Freight was about core business principles: measurements of revenue and control of overheads, those sorts of things. But he had an astounding personal touch. Every staff member of his in the early days who had a first child, or their first child since arriving with the company, got sent a beautiful silver frame to hold a photograph of the child. I was deeply touched when I got mine, and I still absolutely cherish it. Then about five years later he put out a letter effectively saying that the company had got so big and so widespread, it felt like a hollow gesture to him and so on. Awfully sad. And troubling. I felt a pang of concern when he did that. I thought, Wow, this had pride of place on my mantelpiece; the chairman of the company sent me that. It meant a great deal. Stopping that was, to me, a signal of what was to come, and the company went through a downward evolution, a devolution, I suppose, shortly after that.

Then the old man passed away and in that period Emery lost its culture. His son took over, and no criticism intended, but he just wasn't the old man. It still was a good business but it wasn't run from the heart; it was run by the accountants and that is what caused the demise of Emery, in my opinion. His son made a few poor investments and, as an introduction to an amusing anecdote, one was a business called Purolator.

I wrote the son (John Emery junior) a letter in 1982; this was nearly 20 years after I'd been working for them. I can still recall it.

> *Dear Mr Emery,*
> *I just want to pay court to your father and*
> *the company he built and what it meant*
> *to me, and what it taught me. I've just*
> *exceeded $50 million in turnover with a*
> *return of 6 per cent (which is excellent in our*
> *business) and I just wanted you to know that*
> *I don't think I could ever have done this if I*
> *hadn't been employed by your good father.*
> *As it is coming up to Thanksgiving I wonder*
> *if you could read this letter to your family*
> *when you sit down for dinner.*

The remarkable thing? He did!

He wrote back to me, saying, 'Owen, I remember you clearly. You were one of the people who set up our South Pacific team. I read your letter to the entire family at Thanksgiving and there was about 10 seconds of absolute silence, then they got up and clapped in memory of their grandfather.'

He went on to say, 'As an additional note, as you know we bought Purolator, which brought us to our knees. I only wish I could report that I had 6 per cent.'

It was a wonderful letter. Incredible: that feeling of being part of someone's family even though you were, technically, simply an employee.

The sentiment was similar when I wrote my farewell letter to all the staff at OTS once I'd sold the business. It basically said: You are my extended family, I would love to hear from you anytime, here's how you communicate with me for those who don't know. You know, I am concerned.

The incoming investors would not print it.

And I wrote a letter to the new chairman and I said: 'I am entrusting my family to you because you convinced me that you care for people.' And I had a Maori carving made which I sent to him, made by the best carver in New Zealand, Donna Grant, who is Sir Howard Morrison's daughter. She carved entwined koru, which meant this is what one family gives to another when they entrust something they love to the other family. That's how I felt about my thousands and thousands of staff.

So I disagree with CEOs who say that it's too hard to maintain some sense of personal touch in a corporate environment. It's hard, but it's not *too* hard. It's all part of management, whether you're managing people, or the numbers, or any other aspect of your business. I just commit to it: that's how I operate.

As the business grew, what progressively happened, naturally, was that I did less and less detail and I focused on the critical things like financial control: the receivables, cashflow and so on. At one stage I used to read all the sales reports from right around the world. In a company of that size operating in all those territories, that was a lot of reading. I'm fortunate because I can look at a report, and quickly see what's not right, what needs attention. But I had to do less and less of that as time went on. I picked the things that I thought were critical to keep the company running and ensured I had the vision to see what could be happening three to six months ahead and so keep us going in the right direction.

And I had to do that globally, by understanding the individual idiosyncrasies of each country.

Take America, for example. America is a land of enterprise. Americans want to be sold to. Americans want to look at the next opportunity. As a consequence, by and large, it's quite easy to do business in America. There are not any governmental constraints preventing you from starting a company, not the restrictions there are in some of the other countries I operated in. A huge number of new companies are formed each year, and an equally huge number of new companies go bankrupt each year. You have as much chance as the next person, which is, in a lot of ways, the foundation of America, its free enterprise.

My personal belief is that foundation, that mentality, came with the first settlers and got a huge boost when the European Jewish communities immigrated in the late 1800s. Then the Germans and the Italians came, the ones with this incredible hard-work ethic: they rolled their sleeves up. Families got involved. People would lend to people, Jewish people particularly would lend to other Jewish people. They understood in the end that their one bulwark against racism and bigotry was power and money.

America wants to succeed. It's actually ingrained in Americans.

The problem has been an increase, over time, of subdivisions of interest: rural versus urban, the various religious groups, different and opposing national entities, haves and have-nots. All these divisions have arisen out of a group's desire to protect what they have developed. It's still America. As long as they have someone at the helm who allows free trade and global vision and doesn't become blindsided by all that, they will succeed. President Obama is, unfortunately, veering dangerously close to that narrowing of the vision, because he's all about bringing manufacturing back to the United States and out of Asia. He should never have gone that far. He should welcome that foreign input, international expertise. The American people showed their true grit when the Japanese came in and showed them how to build cars properly. What did they do? They fought back. Look at a General Motors car today compared with 30 years ago. America can adapt, can change. It's highly innovative. Look what they do in Silicon Valley, they're light years ahead of everybody. Still.

When Newt Gingrich says he's going to start up a space programme and put a colony on the moon, he would have done it had he been elected. America can do it. Yet they waste a huge amount of money. Why are they fighting all these ridiculous little wars everywhere? Concentrate your energies somewhere else. Make it very difficult for the bad guys to go anywhere or do anything. Have an international blacklist, use other methods.

And the West needs to do more, not just America. Europe is

falling by the wayside. Europeans are curiously super-tolerant of all the errors and omissions they make. Look at the Italians! They've had more governments than there have been years since World War II. The French spend a significant percentage of income taxes on welfare. It's unbelievable. Spain has almost 25 per cent unemployment! Finland, Sweden, Norway and Denmark have structures and policies that are way ahead of the countries in the Mediterranean. Look at the Greeks, they don't even give a stuff. The people who make all the money all have two sets of books. It's a tragedy. Why should other countries in the European Union suffer because of the way Greece runs itself into the ground?

My view is: let Italy go broke, let Greece go broke, let Spain go broke. They can't go on themselves. Then come in with the rules and regulations to make them toe the line. Or toss them out.

I say all this from my business experience. As I've said, it's very, very hard for a foreign company outside of Europe to break into the European psyche in doing business. The preferred way is to buy a company, however defunct it might be, because what you're actually buying, by doing that, is membership of Europe.

Another very important lesson I learned was at Harvard from Professor Marty Marshall. He died a couple of years ago, at age 86. Amazing guy, but a rough diamond. For some reason, he picked out me on this particular occasion, in front of everyone on the entrepreneurs' course.

'I've got a question to ask you: what business are you in?'

'I'm in the non-vessel operating common carrier business.'

'What the hell is that? What the *heck* do you mean?'

'Well, Marty, I don't own ships. People give me their freight to move from one point to another, I put it into containers and I contract to move those containers on ships.'

And he said, 'That's a *business*? You make *money*?' Then he turns to the rest of the class and says, 'Does anyone understand what he's talking about? Thought so. No idea whatsoever.' Then he's back on my case. 'You got phones in your business? When the phone rings and you pick it up, you open the conversation and say "Hello", tell me, what does the other person say?'

And I said, 'Well, if he's a customer he asks me questions. If he's got something to move he'll ask, "When's your next sailing to this destination? What is the rate?" I'll maybe ask him, "Do you have any special packaging requirements?" That sort of thing.'

Marty went, 'So what's he really asking you for?'

'Information.'

'Now, tell me again, what business are you in?'

And I said, 'Marty, I'm in the information business.'

It just fell into place in my head. I thought, My gosh! I am in the information business. From that moment in time the penny dropped. I left that session and went to sit in my room for a while, and I thought, This is where technology comes in, this is where we can get better, more accurate, on time, 24/7 information. That's what we're in, the information business.

He was brilliant. I wrote and thanked him after that session.

So that's what made up my business, then: information.

What particular components make for a successful entrepreneur? I can throw in my two bits' worth and say, well, these are the things that make me what I am, and these are what make me successful. I've tried to do that in this section, to a degree. Ultimately, though, it's hard to put 50 years in business, with all its pitfalls and successes, down to a particular formula, or one set of principles and ideas. One thing I often get asked is, 'What is the one attribute you have that defines you?' Help! I invariably respond with an anecdote from my course at Harvard. I retold it in my acceptance speech when I received my honorary doctorate and it got a few laughs, so it bears repeating here.

One of the professors, Phil Hall, told us this story.

The dean once asked Phil to afternoon tea on a Sunday. Along he went and the dean said, 'Phil, I want you to undertake a project. I want you to find out what makes an entrepreneur tick. Get a team together, whoever you need, and you can use the offices under Baker Library.'

So he went out there and picked a team and they got together and mapped out their programme and process. They held hundreds of interviews, cross-referenced the information, asked the same questions in different ways, covering, they hoped, all the bases. Phil was to go back in six months and report to the dean, which he duly did. He went to the dean who said, 'Well, Phil, do you have anything to tell me?' Phil said, 'Yes, sir, we've come to a conclusion as to what unique attribute it is that entrepreneurs have. We've managed to isolate this and we've brought it down to three letters, R L C.'

At this point, when he was telling us the story, Phil said, 'Thank you all,' and left the podium. Everyone, of course, was hanging out, imploring him to come back. 'What does it stand for, what does it mean?' It was almost like everyone was asking, 'What's the secret formula? What's the secret to life?' Is it some strange mathematical calculation, some scientific equation?

So he returned — great sense of theatre, this guy — and said, almost off-handedly, *'Rat-Like Cunning.'*

Is that what I've got?!

I certainly developed a sixth sense, I think, a way of knowing how to implement the human relations strategies I've talked about, how to read all the nuances in the reports and the numbers, and then trying to see the big picture, see what's coming. I do believe that is God's gift to me, being able to read the signs.

I predicted the big drop in 2008 six months before anybody else in our business. When I started telling people what I believed was coming, they'd ask me why. I'd reply, 'Because the signs aren't right.' I decided to cut back on all expansion, I stopped expenditure on heavy IT expansion, which was really the bells and whistles on a very good system. I said, 'Hang on, we don't need to spend that $10 million, we don't need to open in eastern Europe. We won't buy those four companies we were looking at for $5 million apiece.' So there was a further $20 million. I could, being the 100 per cent shareholder, just tighten up those nuts. Our volumes went down but our margin remained constant. We reduced our overheads: so, happiness.

As soon as it turned around, about 15 months later, we were ready. We just dusted off the programmes, tuned them up a little bit, and off we went. That's what happened in our business.

I did exactly the same thing after September 11. Same principles. And during that period there were certainly some days that were pretty edgy.

But I never saw failure as an option. I mainly thought, Today will be a toughie. But I never gave up. I did my best slugging coming out of the corner. A lot of people have said that. I suppose you could say it's an underdog mentality. If people say or think I can't do it or I won't survive: that motivates me completely.

Partly I think that comes from leaving school at 15, reacting to my background. A lot of it was a challenge to myself.

That's one thing I *do* still lament, though, the fact that I didn't have the opportunity to go to university. I would've without doubt been in the debating club and the chess club. I like playing chess. And I think like that in business; I think five moves ahead. I'll get where I need to go but when I take the next move I'll often say, 'Oops, you're not going to get there that way, pal.' I just think that way. I always have plan B in place, always. Some people might find that surprising, because the perception of entrepreneurs is often that they 'win at all costs' and they just persist until they get there. But you also have to assess a situation and know if it's *not* going to work and, if so, how to exit as quickly as you can.

When I see a situation that I consider too hard and not worth the time and effort, I will switch and take another point of view; I amend my point of view to suit. I don't push it against all the odds. I'm never that right. I'd like to feel I'm not often wrong either, though.

Some people refuse to change course because they think that's the ultimate in self-belief, to keep pushing. But that's just ego. There's no room for ego in successful enterprises. That may sound like a contradiction, so I'll clarify.

While you need that determination and self-belief, there's good and bad ego. The good ego is when you believe you can do it with or without help, normally with help. Bad ego is when you think you're so right that you'll trample on anybody else's opinions to get there. That is bad. Because even if you win the day you're standing out there alone.

My favourite expression, which I included in my acceptance speech for the honorary doctorate, is from Theodore Roosevelt: 'Far better it is to dare mighty things, to win glorious triumphs even though checkered by failure, than to rank with those poor spirits who neither enjoy nor suffer much because they live in the grey twilight that knows neither victory nor defeat.' Marvellous, wonderful words. I saw that nearly 40 years ago on someone's desk and it captivated me. I asked the guy whose desk it was on to send me a copy and he did. It sits on my desk in my villa in Fiji, in the office. I think that absolutely sums up what I believe.

People bemoan mediocrity, and I do too, but, in a way, mediocrity can be a stepping stone to success. You can either move up or you can fail but I always say, don't just stand there immobile. Ultimately the vision, inspiration and readiness to accept a challenge often come from a very small number of people.

Ultimately, the drive in me to be successful and to give my kids a good education forced me to keep going and to be better at what I did. The only thing I knew I had to do was sell myself: that was it. When I boarded an aircraft I talked to the guy next to me. When I was waiting in an airport I talked to somebody. When I went to a business meeting I didn't just talk about business, I asked all sorts of questions. People are interested in talking to me because I am interested in talking to them. I learned a lot through other people.

And I'd do my research, my homework. Before I had an important meeting with someone, I'd find out as much as I could about that person. And this was before Google! An example is a meeting I had with a company called Abbott Labs. I remember going to see them in their boardroom in Milwaukee. I asked them to send me the annual report and I read it before I even got to the States. I got information from another source about what Abbott's shares were doing. Basically I was armed when we met and I could talk to them. They were amazed I knew this stuff. I'd bring it gently into the discussion.

They said, 'You've done a bit of homework, Mr Glenn.'

I said, 'I care about your business and if I don't understand your business I can't be any help to you.'

They looked at each other and looked at me and I could tell they were thinking, Is this guy bullshitting us? But it's what sold them.

Because a lot of people, a lot of businesses, they don't do that. They don't do their homework, they don't bother finding out about you before they come to talk to you. And when they do come to talk to you, at you, they don't really care what you're thinking. They don't care whether or not you understand what they're saying.

I sell by the pauses; when I don't speak in negotiation, that's when I'm winning. I can remember times when the silences have been long and strained. I just sit there. Scribble a few notes. I'm waiting for an answer and I'm not going to say another word. They'll speak first and that's it. That's how I felt I could win the argument or win the moment.

I always tried to bring something different to the negotiations. I went to visit a company out in the Midlands. I looked around the office and saw a table tennis trophy. I said to the guy I was seeing, who was in his early fifties, 'Do you still play?'

'Yeah, down the club,' he replied.

ABOVE | My mother at Ellerslie Racecourse, Auckland in 2006.

BELOW | My sixty-third 'sports fancy dress' birthday party at the Loaded Hog at Auckland's Viaduct. I went dressed as a female rugby player and Mum asked, 'Who is this person?'

ABOVE | With Sister Declan Fahy, a Cluny nun in Kalimpong. In her final years, Sister Declan was in charge of the Cluny Women's College where the Glenn Family Foundation built the Declan Hall.

BELOW | At the school in Macau, singing 'You Are My Sunshine'.

ABOVE | With good friends Jimmy Keir, Johnny Anslow and
Mal Gordon at the Beijing Olympics.

BELOW | Unveiling my portrait at Auckland Business School. L–R: Mal
Gordon, brother Mike Glenn, Prof. Greg Whittred and Johnny Anslow.

ABOVE | Presenting the 2009 Glenn Family Foundation Kiwi Cup: the disabled sailors trophy.

BELOW | With two of the disabled sailors competing in the Kiwi Cup.

ABOVE | A visit to see 'my children' in Kalimpong in 2011; also in the photo are my daughter Sue and PA, Denni.

BELOW | A proud dad with daughters Jenny, Sue and Catherine in Fiji.

RIGHT | With Black Sticks Women co-captains Emily Naylor (left) and Kayla Sharland (right), 2011.

BELOW | With Leandro Negre, President of the FIH, at the Owen Glenn Champions Trophy in Auckland, December 2011.

LEFT | Chris. My sixth child and only son.

BELOW | With Hugh Fletcher after receiving our honorary doctorates from the University of Auckland, February 2012.

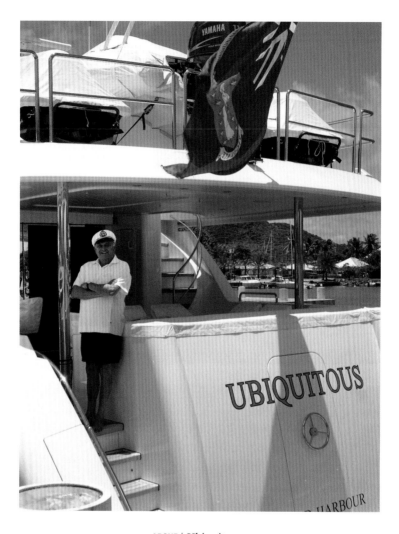

ABOVE | *Ubiquitous.*

I said, 'Okay, tell you what, you look like a gambling man, you're weighing up EMG [a competitor] against us. You've got a couple of bats and a ball, let's put the books across the boardroom table as the net. I'll play you for it. Best of 11.'

He won. He was bloody good!

He said, 'I don't believe I just did that.' He thought for a bit and said, 'But really, I'm just back where I started.'

I said, 'Oh well, at least we had a bit of fun.'

He gave me a part of the business. Everybody else tried to sell to them; I didn't.

Ironically, while I showed a lot of confidence there, that was when I was working for MSAS who, by getting rid of me in the manner they did (see Chapter 2), absolutely destroyed my confidence for a while. It was a huge, huge blow. What knocked me most was that I felt that the company had been utterly disloyal to me. I put heart, soul, lungs, everything into that business. I hired most of the people. Then, through what I would describe as office politics, someone came along and was able to change all that. They had the guts to apologise three years later. They said to me, 'Oh look, we did you a favour.'

One thing that came from it was that it took me a while to trust an English businessman again.

"

It's a national malaise: 'Will my life be disturbed if I make that decision? Probably. Then I'm not going to make it.' How did this inertia happen?

"

CHAPTER 8 —
SETTING A HIGHER BENCHMARK

I THINK I'M REALLY JUST TOO MUCH OF A LONER TO BE A PUBLIC SERVANT.

I am often asked, usually when I'm having a bit of a rant about something that frustrates or disappoints me about the way New Zealand is being run or the direction it's going in: Why don't you enter politics? Or, more commonly, Why *didn't* you enter politics?

Overall, I have no political ambitions. There's the obvious reason: I have poured all my time and energy into two things, business and philanthropy. Second, I don't think I could handle the lack of integrity in the political arena. Third, I'm too old! If I'd taken an interest 20 years ago, even 15, maybe, *maybe* then, but I haven't got the patience to become part of a political party. On top of that, I think I'm really just too much of a loner to be a public servant. However, I am very interested in economic policy and how it affects our country.

Looking at all of the past political parties in New Zealand, at their threadbare policies, I don't really see enough substance. But we get the government we deserve. It's a national malaise: 'Will my life be disturbed if I make that decision? Probably. Then I'm not going to make it.' How did this inertia happen?

When we finally came out from under the aprons of Mother England, we struggled to find out what the hell we were and who we were. It was only when England and the Common Market turned its back on New Zealand in the early 1970s that we were forced to do something about that. So we created government departments and government-heavy organisations like the Lamb Marketing Board and the Dairy Board, and now we have Fonterra.

In my opinion Fonterra could double its revenue if it marketed its products with more vigour. Instead it is driven to simply achieve an increase over the previous year's results. The western world is finally looking at poverty properly, and looking at problems in Africa and other developing nations. There are huge amounts of money that are available globally to basically feed the starving, and there is no shortage of undernourished people, it's painful to say. Fonterra, clearly, makes products that meet those needs. We could sell such products through a

UN fund. Are we doing that? If not, why not?

In a general sense, I think we went too far down the socialist path in this country. It was an overflow from industrial Britain through their successive Labour governments. We just became a country that operated on the basis that we didn't have to earn a living, that Britain would buy everything we produced, which they did. When the European Economic Community was formed, it really hit everybody in the guts. Suddenly we had to find other markets, but it didn't change our socialist status. The government said, 'We'll just borrow the money, we'll trade out of it.' The funny thing is New Zealand *did* trade out of it many times . . . and it just continued spending beyond its means. Spend more and get more back and then spend more. Austerity was never part of our national make-up. Hot pie, cold beer, couple of bob to put on the gee-gees, no sweat.

It doesn't breed aspiration, a willingness to better yourself. Why would you bother? If you've got a hot pie and a cold beer, hell, what else is there? A pair of shorts and jandals. I don't think, in general, that New Zealanders are lazy people, I don't at all, I just think we fit in and if the community we live in doesn't set a higher benchmark, everyone just conforms. So often New Zealanders don't aspire to better their lot.

And while I do believe that's partly a hangover from our British background, the funny thing about the Aussies is they're not like that. They came out below decks so they were always challenging authority and the norm. Aussies have a far stronger attitude towards making things happen, whether it's on the sports field, in business, whatever you care to name. They're our cousins just some 2000 kilometres away but the attitudes of the people are totally different.

New Zealand is struggling with that ill-informed promise that it's going to match Australia in years to come. They're going away faster than we're growing up. It's never going to happen. Show me what New Zealand is going to do to increase its GDP to the extent that it will match Australia's. And yet United Nations statistics state that we're the world's second-richest country in terms of natural resources per capita, all under the ground — oil, gas, minerals. We are second only to Saudi Arabia in terms of our natural capital per capita. It's an absolutely amazing statistic. So my argument is: Look, if we do allow somebody a permit to explore our waters and find a gas field and it's 250 kilometres offshore and they build a platform, exactly whose view are we impeding?!

I realise some may consider the term 'responsible drilling' to be a touch ambiguous, but if we apply rigorous and well-researched science and technology to the processes, as we have done with both agribusiness and manufacturing, I firmly believe that we can proceed confidently in the exploration of this 'gold mine' under our feet. We don't want a repeat in this country of the Gulf of Mexico disaster; nor can we possibly put lives at risk, or have the dreadful tragedy that was Pike River reoccurring in this sector. Permitting responsible organisations only to get involved in the exploration of our mineral wealth — and these are easily vetted to strict criteria — is one very simple, tangible and effective way of ensuring any investigations are done in a way that is sympathetic to all our resources: our people, our land, our environment. Responsible exploration of renewable resources could generate huge gains in jobs and growth. It's irresponsible not to pursue this to some degree.

Two crucial factors are required to make this happen: political will and courage from the government, and buy-in and belief from the public. The noise that has built up around the current government's proposed partial asset sales shows that certainly the second of these characteristics is in short supply on this particular issue and, while the government has shown some political courage and stuck to its guns over this one, political will and stamina are not the usual stock-in-trade of any government or political party. I hope the National Government holds its course on the asset sales strategy. Why?

If 'selling the family silver', as opponents of this strategy like to term it, actually produces some real 'gold', in terms of a return on investment, then it makes political sense. The same concerns about what sits on the negative side of the accounting ledger, which makes responsible mining exploration a winner, apply here too. We need to fund a phenomenally expensive rebuild in Christchurch, we have a wealth of leaky home payouts to deal with. Our ageing population, as it will in most of the developed world, is going to become an increasing and ongoing financial burden to the rest of the country. And there's a billion dollars' worth of Treaty settlements in the offing, at last count. To those who ply the public sentiment for opposition to both these sound economic plans for no other reason than column inches and perceived political gain, I say, shame on you.

Despite the 'zero budget' the government's debt is monumental. Our private debt figures are even more frightening; depending on which statistics you look at, New Zealanders owe more per capita than the US$50,000 (and rising) that saddles the neck of every American citizen. What's even more concerning about this level of private debt is that much of it has been used to finance non-productive assets in property markets. Put these two financial facts together, the public and the private debt levels, and the picture is woeful. Partial privatisation and responsible mineral exploration are two very clear ways of heading away from this position of unacceptable indebtedness and moving towards a self-supporting, responsible society. We need these sorts of practical steps from our employees in the Beehive and no one with a conscience and a belief in this country should shoot them down in flames when they float such ideas. At least consider them, surely?

I would go much further than mere consideration, natural-ly. I would implement these strategies and once the returns began to materialise, as they would, I would look closely at how we allocate the funds. Yes, as I've just said, the mountain of debt needs to be addressed. But, as they're starting to say in Europe, 'austerity' and debt reduction are not the only drivers of growth. Even with the financial albatross around the neck of every New Zealander, we need to invest as well. We need to look for investment opportunities that will directly help individual New Zealanders, the ones who are working hard and using their abilities to progress themselves and the country, in whatever sector they're operating in. We support them, and get the rest of the country in behind them. And we move forward.

Do we keep ploughing (!) money into agriculture, the tired old mainstay, the fallback provider for New Zealand Inc.?

Yes! Agriculture and the related food industries are a huge part of this country's competitive advantage. Agriculture and forestry account for approximately 65 per cent of this country's exports, and the world, right now, is screaming for quality food products from reputable, that is safe, producers. I've said it before: Here's our chance to be the mouse that roared. We have a well-deserved worldwide reputation in agribusiness — if we really work at twinning that with the technological expertise we have in this country, surely we could become unstoppable in this area? What if Massey University worked more closely with Crown Research Institutes to keep on finding those niches that we are so good at exploring and turning to our advantage? What if there was an institute, along the lines of the very successful ICEHOUSE model at the University of Auckland, that combined science and technology with agribusiness research, that showed a commitment of resources and intent in this area, that helped establish products and processes that were saleable on a global scale, that was capable of producing a real and ongoing economic return for the country? Science writer Julian Cribb has said that New Zealand has the potential to become 'the Silicon Valley of agricultural knowledge' — and he's absolutely right. Imagine it. What would that look like? New Zealand needs to profitably connect with the world if it wants to be a highly successful small country and trading force. And these are ways it can do that.

Of course we need the educational environment to help develop this in the first place. My investment in the University of Auckland Business School and the AUT Millennium Institute of Health and Sport was to encourage this type of framework, one of educational excellence, and to explore and develop the potential inherent in our bright young people. It is shameful that we spend so little on research and development compared with most OECD countries: our finest entrepreneurial minds should be encouraged, not made to strike out on their own in spite of the environment in which they are trying to succeed.

It's vital that the average New Zealander receives the exposure or experience that they need to keep them challenged, to keep their intellect developing, to ensure they reach their potential. We need to ask ourselves: Do we have the right environment here? The figures say (all the time) that up to 25 per cent of good Kiwis have left the country, and they're the ones who have done the hard yards, developed their intellect, reached their potential. When you talk to people like Sir John Buchanan or Sir Douglas Myers, people like that, you have a different level of conversation. These people *know*. They have done battle in the international marketplace.

Of course, not everyone who leaves New Zealand becomes globally significant or amazingly successful but, generally speaking, New Zealanders are considered good employees, trustworthy people to deal with, not as brash as the Aussies but that doesn't matter. What's of concern is the widening knowledge and experience gap between New Zealand and elsewhere. The rest of the world is striding ahead, and we are not keeping pace.

I never want to be someone who only shouts from the sidelines. While I will do that — and the series of articles I wrote for the *New Zealand Herald* in 2011 was exactly that — what I prefer to do is take meaningful action. I am also aware that there are already existing channels there to ostensibly change things for the better, such as government, so I have done my utmost to talk to whoever is in power and offer some suggestions. I have said, 'Look, we can harness Kiwis overseas, we really can, but we've got to give them a blueprint to work with.'

Kiwi Expatriates Abroad (KEA) strives to do this and needs our support; well done Sir Stephen Tindall.

I talked to the CEO of New Zealand Trade and Enterprise (NZTE) and he accepted the point and said he is trying to change things for the better. I believe him. I said to him, 'Let's take China as an example. You don't have to employ just New Zealanders in NZTE positions: employ good Chinese people. It's easy for them to come to New Zealand, have a good look around and discover what we're all about and take that back. As well, the best place to recruit from is the ex-alumni of our universities who are now back home. There are thousands of them. What great ambassadors they could be.'

He liked it. And that's where some of the recruits already come from. These are the people who love New Zealand, they've come through our education system and succeeded; they have benefited from an education here. They know what the All Blacks and Warriors mean, they know what decent dairy food tastes like. These are the people who have some affiliation, some loyalty and some belief that New Zealand has credibility.

There's an intelligentsia in New Zealand, not more than 12–15 per cent, who do care and who really want to understand and really want to make a difference. But the government doesn't see any need to appeal to those people and rally them to this cause. What about forming a think-tank? I'm a starter!

In general, I believe the government has become frustrated about poverty and child abuse and everything that goes with those problems. Have we grown to accept it? This country's record in child abuse is a national disgrace. We have the fifth-highest rate in the OECD: a child dies of child abuse in New

Zealand *every five weeks*; a child under two is admitted to hospital with preventable injuries *every five days*. Let's add in that we have the second-highest rate of teenage pregnancies in the world, with only the US taking top honours in this area. Our suicide rate for 15–19-year-olds is the highest in the OECD and double that of Australia.

Now, I know from personal experience, having invested heavily in community development projects in impoverished areas around the world, that there are a raft of complex issues behind these statistics. But we cannot let those issues, or the great Kiwi 'she'll be right' attitude, blind us to our responsibilities.

We must do something. We can't leave it solely up to the government, and I'll talk about this in the next chapter, as I am hugely passionate about putting this right.

Now something dominated life in New Zealand during my time down here in 2011, dominated the headlines more than it usually does, and that was rugby. I'm okay with that. It's well documented: I'm a rugby nut. I love the All Blacks. I've watched them play all over the world. But there needs to be a sense of balance. There's nothing wrong with following sport, it's a healthy outlet and good for the country if we achieve recognition. But why can't we put the same sense of purpose and determination into trade and products? The Aussies have a far greater identification with pushing Australia. Australia Made, the lovely little kangaroo. We need stronger country brand identification. We used to have it, but it's lost visibility.

There simply aren't the crusaders out there. I don't criticise to embarrass anyone; I'm just asking, Why don't we look at this?

One thing I very much like about the United States is that you can come from anywhere in the world but if you get American citizenship you are *an American*. Whether your origins are in China or Nigeria, it doesn't matter. I believe in New Zealand there is still a lingering bigotry. Australia suffers from it a little, too. Where its attitude towards Aborigines is concerned, Australia is guilty as charged, no question; but the era of the White Australia policies has passed and everyone needs to move on.

Maori have shown far greater resilience and anger than the Aborigines in insisting their language and heritage be protected and I certainly don't blame them for that. What I worry about is Maori feeling they're so different that we get to a place where Maori are first and New Zealand is second.

Sir Howard Morrison and I used to have fierce arguments about this; I don't deny that I used to provoke him!

Howie said to me, 'You don't understand Maori history.'

My message to Maori is simply this: I'd just like you to think you're New Zealanders first. Yes, you've got grievances and, yes, they should be resolved, but let's resolve them once and for all. Let's close the book. In the end you'll cause division. Howie never accepted that point of view from me. Never. His heart was in the right place but he couldn't see that change is necessary for us to move forward as one country.

I believe certain iwi elders have feathered their nests at the expense of their own people, particularly their people who so desperately need assistance both economically and from a health perspective. Instead of working with the troubled communities, they buy buildings, they buy sports clubs and they deny their own people opportunities to flourish. They're amassing more wealth as they go along. Even if they subdivided the wealth and gave every person in the iwi a share . . .

When a percentage of commercial fishing rights was restored to Maori, Rex George, who used to coach for me at Belmont Shore Rugby Club in California and had been captain of the Maori All Blacks, emailed me and said, 'I've just received a letter telling me I'm entitled to all these fishing rights. What on earth do I do with them?'

I sent him back two words, 'Go fishing.'

He had no idea what the rights meant; it wasn't practical in any day-to-day sense.

I bring that up only in the context of being a Kiwi. I believe we are a multicultural society and that is a huge advantage but we need to integrate Maori culture, not isolate it.

Howard said to me once, 'You know, Owen, I'm actually 85 per cent Scottish.'

I said, 'Aren't you proud of your Scottish heritage?'

'Not as much as I am of my Maori heritage.'

Isn't that interesting?

As for the Winston Peters debate, all I want to do here is put the facts straight once and for all.

I was very naïve when I backed the Labour Party. I will admit that. I hadn't been in New Zealand and I thought Helen Clark had the tiller in her hand and that New Zealand wasn't doing nearly as badly as I finally found out it was. I didn't realise just how heavily the Labour Government was borrowing to prop up New Zealanders' standard of living and the welfare programme.

So why did I do it? Why did I give them money?

For the record, they didn't ask me.

I met Helen at a tourism function that the New Zealand Government was sponsoring in Sydney.

So, because I thought they were doing a good job, I offered to support them.

A few weeks later Mike Williams (then Labour Party president) contacted me and we met in Sydney. I agreed to donate $500,000.

Over a period of two years we met in New Zealand, Australia and the South of France, and Mike raised with me my ongoing interest in New Zealand and politics.

Given my business connections, I was constantly rubbing shoulders with influential people, including royalty and various government associates from around the world. My initial thought was, How can I make this work for New Zealand?

What I had in mind was an ambassador at large role, but completely at my expense; at no point did I expect the government to contribute — that was never the idea.

If the ambassador at large role didn't appeal, I thought I could host New Zealand trade delegates in Monaco as an honorary consul, bring a rugby Sevens tournament there, be a contact for New Zealanders if they needed assistance when visiting Monaco, again with no financial assistance from the government. While I had been invited to the palace in Monaco, the reality was in order to have credibility with the palace and other official channels, I would of course need an endorsement from the New Zealand Government.

Mike said he would speak to Helen Clark and it was then referred to Winston Peters as Foreign Minister.

I then met with Winston in Sydney at his request and again

when he was in France for an All Black rugby test. He said to me they had decided they didn't need such a role. I outlined to him the ideas I had and told him it would be at no cost to New Zealand, and he said he would ask his bureaucrats again.

Then in the 2005 election he lost his seat in Tauranga and he contacted me asking for assistance with his legal fees of $100,000. Within minutes of speaking to him I had an email from his lawyer with the details of his bank account to pay the money into.

Meanwhile, Mike Williams contacted me and asked for a further $100,000 for new computers, which I agreed to provide in the form of a loan, to be repaid within the following 12 months. I discussed with him the approach I'd had from Winston and he came back to me and said he'd talked it over 'with the powers that be', and there was no objection. So I paid the money to Winston's lawyers.

I actually felt a bit of a fool that I'd given the Labour Party the money. But what really turned me against them was that I felt they lacked integrity.

Winston saying he never received any support from me and my then having to come down to New Zealand and prove that he had — well, it was done to death in the newspapers and you'd know all about it from reading them. Or at least whatever bits of it the media wanted to tell. If you don't know what I'm referring to, you're lucky! A very small episode in my life.

The overall lesson for New Zealand, whether you know, understand or believe the details or not, is how can a country elect someone who, when he held the privileged portfolio of Foreign Minister, was found by his peers to have effectively misled the House? Where is our self-respect as a nation, that we would let that man hold a role in our Parliament again? Extraordinary.

"

I know from experience that even when your situation looks absolutely hopeless, there is always a way out.

"

CHAPTER 9 —
GIVING PEOPLE A LEG-UP

'MY SON, GOD WILL PROVIDE. BUT SOMETIMES HE'S A LITTLE SLOW AND THAT'S WHY I'M ASKING YOU.'

I started giving away money when I was about 26 — even when I really didn't have any! Why? I guess I have always felt that to have a meaningful existence you have an obligation to help those who can't help themselves. That's the principal driver behind the Glenn Family Foundation, which I established in the 1980s.

On top of that, I have assisted on a case-by-case basis,

helping people in situations I empathise with, such as custody battles with kids and angry ex-wives, or giving people a leg-up when their perspective is that they're in an untenable position. Often helping them at that point just brings them into the light a little bit, changes their viewpoint, so from there on in, they can actually help themselves.

I know from experience that even when your situation looks absolutely hopeless, or you've just taken a beating and the way ahead looks impossible, there is, in fact, always, *always* a path ahead, always a way out. Sometimes I've helped provide that when people haven't been able to do it for themselves.

I get a lot of requests for a whole range of donations. I've decided to go this way. Education, sports, the environment: they attract me. And the child abuse and domestic violence issues are where I can make a difference.

So there's the Glenn Family Foundation, a global organisation that helps the needy, and part of the reason for my selling OTS when I did was so I could focus my energies on the work the Foundation does. Then there's personal philanthropy, as I've just explained: people who, for whatever reason, cross my path and have a need that I can help them with. Then, and there's a separate chapter devoted to this, there's my new initiative to combat the horrendous statistics that reflect the child abuse situation in New Zealand, which we've called, Help: Make a Difference. That phrase sums up what I've tried to do my entire life when it comes to giving. There's no point in giving — to a cause or an individual — unless you are somehow going to make a difference in their lives. Tagged on to this is the hope that you've empowered them in some way, enabled them to then help *themselves*, get *themselves* ahead and, in turn, help someone else.

Here's a good example.

One of the villages in Kalimpong, where we do a great deal of work through the Foundation, is a pretty little place called Bong Busty. My man there, Saom Namchu, has done an amazing job with our Model Village Programme, where we work on making a difference to sanitation, water, education, basic needs, that sort of thing. One of the things I did at Bom Busty was that I gave the villagers domestic animals. They had a choice of pigs, cows, chickens or goats. Now this one guy, who I'm thinking of to illustrate my point, he used to walk 90 minutes every day down into the valley, to the river where he worked for 10 hours breaking stones, and then spent 90 minutes walking home again. He did this every day of his life. No breaks. To make matters worse, he hardly made enough to feed his children.

So, he was persuaded to take a cow. Now these are very special, hardy, high-production cows and part of the deal was that if they took the cow, we built them a concrete cowpen, complete with sanitation and suchlike. He took his cow, and then came back eight months later to tell Saom how he'd got on.

He got up and said, 'I have done well with this cow. One-third of its milk production I use to give my extended family milk, one-third I use to make milk products and cheese to sell, and one-third I give to the village. And now I've saved enough money to buy a second cow.'

Saom got up and said, 'Well, now you may understand why when Mr Glenn built the cowpen he built it for two cows.'

True story. The man didn't have to break stones any more. He started a business and then he got his family involved in growing vegetables and he became self-sufficient. *That's* the point of philanthropy.

As I mentioned earlier in the book, when we came over from India to Auckland, we continued going to Catholic schools, likely because my father was under pressure from my Aunt Marion, a devout Catholic.

Now I believe that the Catholics drum into you that you've got to be educated in a Catholic school for a number of reasons, all their own, but it's mainly because they want to expand the flock. When my father withdrew us the priest said to him, 'You can't do that, you can't just pull your boys out of the school.'

They actually told us we'd go to hell!

My father who, as I've said, was a man of few words but when he spoke, you listened, said to the priest, 'Look. The first time I've even seen or heard from you is when we withdrew our children from your school. Every time we went to church, all you talked about was raising money. There's no proper sermon, it's all money, money, money to build this and do that. I had to give my children five different coins to put in various collection plates. I'm not going to suffer under this yoke.'

That was that. He prevailed. See, in my mind, that wasn't about loving God; that was about extortion!

My dear father. One of my first philanthropic exercises involved my father. Even when I had little or nothing, I always helped my parents, and this is a good example. I retell it not because I want to look good, but because, I believe, it's a delightful story and it gave me so much pleasure to be able to repay my father in kind, for some of what he did for me.

It happened when I was first living in England. I was 28 or so, and had two kids and one on the way. I'd come out to New Zealand from London, just visiting really, and we were getting ready to go out somewhere and my father pulled out the one suit he had. I got very emotional just seeing that, and realising that my father had not had a new suit for 10 years. I just thought, Poor old Dad. He'd suffered health problems and couldn't hold a meaningful job down, so I was helping my parents, which I was pleased to be able to do, but I just thought, What else can I do for Dad? Which got me thinking . . .

So I wrote to Hugh Wright's in Queen Street, who were the main men's clothing retailer at the time.

I said to them, 'I want to do something for my father, I'd like to invite him to come in to get a made-to-measure suit.' Which was really something in those days. 'I don't want him to know about this, so I'm going to arrange for a friend to pick him up and bring him in to be measured, so he can select the cloth and so forth. Would you do this for me and tell me how much it all will cost?'

I got a letter back from the managing director confirming all the details. (Brief deviation: I saw one of his descendants in London last year when the vice chancellor from the University of Auckland came over and Dougie Myers threw a dinner. This guy's name was Wright — as you'd expect! — and he was the great-grandson of the original Hugh Wright. I told him this story and he was fascinated. See how the ripples spread on the pond?)

I organised a friend of the family to pick up Dad and take him into the store. He was great. He said to Dad, 'Oh let's just wander around.' My dad didn't do that sort of thing and he was wondering what the hell was going on.

Hugh Wright's guys were waiting and they came over and said, 'You're Mr Glenn? Good. Come with us.'

The master tailor was ready. He explained to my father what it was all about, and Dad was very touched, shed a few tears. They measured him and he chose a fabric. He came back for two fittings; he got his suit. The next time I came out from England he met me at the airport in the suit. Proud as punch! What a moment!

The other time I was able to help in a specific way was the day when the old family car had to be sold. Dad had just got so sick and they needed the money. He didn't think they could possibly replace it. I knew he really wanted a Triumph. So I gave him the cash. I remember the amount was £700. It was a brand-new car.

Dad and Mum went in to the dealership, and were looking around. He saw this car he wanted and said to the salesman, 'What colours have you got and when can it be delivered?'

And they said, 'If you like this car in this colour it's available now and we could have it ready for you in the morning. Subject to finance, of course.'

My father said to my mother, 'What do you think?' Followed swiftly by, 'We'll take it.'

'Would you like to come to the office, sir, we'll have to make application for finance.'

'Oh no,' said my father, 'I'm paying cash.'

My father didn't have any money but because I'd sent him some, he had the cash in his pocket. He put the cash down.

My mother said to me later, 'You should have seen his face.'

Family aside, I've gone in to bat for many, many people. You have to. I remember one particular instance well. One of our warehousemen in Chicago was someone I'd never actually met, but I'd been told he was having a really tough job getting to see his kids. His wife divorced him and was, as I'd experienced, using the kids. His case was coming up and he couldn't afford representation. I thought, Bugger that, and let it be known through his manager that I would pay all his legal fees. Personally. He could've got it through the public system but I said, 'Get him the best lawyer you can get.' And he won the right to see his kids. He wrote me a nice note in pencil on some ruled paper, but that's actually not the point.

I've just done it for a guy from India who was in IT in LA. Same thing, the wife had ignored court orders and everything. I said to his boss, 'Look, here's $20,000 he can spend. I want him to have access to his kids.' He got it. It's justice.

Hardly anybody knows about these two things. I didn't tell anybody. Why would I? Mostly I do it for the kids. These families need their dad. I went through that and it was a horror story.

What drives my philanthropy in general? It just comes naturally to me. My mother was over-generous, which I am a bit. Maybe it's her fault! The first major contribution I made to any organisation was when my mate Jimmy Keir, in Hong Kong, introduced me to the Caritas Catholics. They're the Catholic order we work with in Macau. I'm so pleased to be able to say that we've made a huge difference.

In the early 1970s, when I first got involved, they had one classroom in Macau with nearly 50 children in it, staffed by one teacher with a Chinese girl as an aid. Now 35 years later I think they have 3400 students in the school and their night classes accommodate 1600 students. All from that one classroom.

One of the people I worked with was Father Luis Ruiz

Suárez, a Spanish Jesuit priest who arrived in China in 1941. At the end of the decade he was expelled from China because of the political situation and, having contracted typhoid, spent time in Macau to recover his health. He stayed on and developed remarkable charitable work in the area, including founding Caritas Macau. We started working with him in the late 1970s. He said something absolutely wonderful to me once, 'My son, God will provide. But sometimes he's a little slow and that's why I'm asking you.'

I'd made a bit of money when he first approached me, not that much, but I said, 'What are you looking for, Father?' He showed me the plans for a nine-storey building to house the elderly. I went back in the 1980s to see this building and it was lovely. I had contributed about 20 per cent of total costs, I think, and the government and other people had helped as well. I was standing outside in the car park and I said, 'Gosh Father, you must really be proud of yourself.' I looked up at it and I said, 'But Father, there's only eight floors.'

And he said, 'Ah, my son, the builder, he kept the ninth floor.'

We're still heavily involved with Caritas today. We support the leper colonies and hospitals for the mentally disabled in China.

Father Ruiz died last year at the age of 97 and Mother Mary, who we'd worked with from the beginning, died the year before at 98. They were saints. I truly believe that. Wonderful, wonderful people. They were a great inspiration to me.

I remember meeting up with Father Ruiz in 2006 and at 92 he used to ride around Macau on a motor scooter. Can you believe that?! We were having a cup of tea in the sanctuary and I said, 'Now, tell me, Father, how is your scooter?'

And he said, 'Oh, my son, we had to retire the scooter. It got old.'

He had a great sense of humour.

Despite the work that Caritas Catholic did in Macau and the difficult circumstances in which they did it, they were always upbeat. They didn't just say it was in God's hands — although they did say that often enough! — but they did a million things to make it work. It's that whole 'God moves mountains but bring a shovel' mentality.

Everywhere Father Ruiz went, particularly going into the hospital where there were a lot of poor patients who had all sorts of mental disabilities, they'd all grab his hand.

Both he and Mother Mary would say, 'They want me to touch them, they want to feel like human beings.'

When he first got involved with the lepers in China, Father Ruiz said, 'My son, there were people we found living in caves, no fresh water, no sanitation. Villagers would go to the mouths of the caves and leave food. In fact, I had to be carried up by porters just to get to them.'

So he raised the money from many people and he built facilities for these people. The Chinese Government would never acknowledge they had a leprosy problem. Never. But because he was doing something about a problem that didn't exist, so to speak, he was allowed to travel freely. He had a pass from Beijing that had been signed by the government.

The politicians and government agents treated him with great respect even though they didn't recognise religion and they didn't recognise leprosy. But Father Ruiz could come and go as he pleased.

And he came and went all over the place, right through

southern China and up into central China. He simply found more and more leper colonies wherever he went. While they say there's no religion in China, there are Catholic priests throughout the country and so he had a network of contacts who were tolerated as long as they kept their heads down. The authorities let him do what he did because they really respected his good work. So maybe there's hope in the end. Dear Father Ruiz, he was so proud of all this.

Mother Mary was amazing. She was a big woman, Italian, the second of five sisters. At her ninetieth birthday, all of her sisters were alive. She hadn't seen them for 40 years or so. I heard through the grapevine that Caritas had, on her birthday, offered her a trip back to Italy to see them all but, being who she was and how she was, she said she didn't want to waste the money. So, in a devious manner, I got my mate Jimmy Keir to talk to Paul Chi Meng Pun, who was the administrator, who we asked to tell Mother Mary that someone had made a donation of the ticket. Would she accept it?

She said she would as long as it wasn't using Caritas funds.

So, on the day of her flight, she went over to Hong Kong on the ferry, Jimmy and Paul picked her up and took her to the airport where the Cathay Pacific airport manager and other people met her and took her to the first-class lounge. She said, 'They're fussing, They're fussing.' She went on board and was taken to first class and of course she said she couldn't sit there. We were ready for that.

She was told it was the only seat left and if she got off the plane the money would be wasted. She had to stay then and they really looked after her. Then Jimmy told her that it was my gift to her. She wrote me a letter telling me I was a very naughty boy.

Mother Mary got off the plane at Rome and had to go up to northern Italy by train. Every step of the way she was monitored and looked after, and she had a wonderful time with her family. They all came together in the way only Italian families can. She just revelled in it all, God bless her.

When she became ill she was moved back to Hong Kong, to the Caritas school and retirement home there. I went to see her on a trip. Even when she was ailing, she'd organised the girls in the domestic classes to bake biscuits for me. She gave me a little statue of the Virgin Mary and a rosary. She was so thoughtful, always.

She was suffering but she said, 'I'm very annoyed Mother Superior has insisted I leave Macau and come here. I refused to go.'

Jimmy said they only convinced her to go to the retirement home by telling her the Mother Superior had conceded that as soon as she got better she could go back.

As soon as I met her on that visit I could see she was up to something and I said to her, 'What are you doing here, Mother Mary?'

'Oh I'm translating the history of the order from Portuguese. They've got me really working here. Goodness knows what's happening to my flock in Macau.'

She was so wily, though. When I gave them donations, Mother Mary would usually say, 'Thank you, my son, God will bless you for this.' But I remember one time in particular; on this instance she said, 'Now, may I ask how much I have to spend to look after my people?'

And I said, 'Oh I thought you and Father Ruiz simply divided it up.'

'Oh no, no, Owen, Father Ruiz has his *own* flock.'

I checked with Jimmy who confirmed that they operated separately. I said to him, 'How do we divvy it up?'

'Fifty-fifty or we'll have World War III!'

There was a rivalry between her and Father Ruiz but a deep, deep love and respect, too. It was really something.

Their spiritual strength was a huge lesson to me. It brought me back to being a good Christian. I have a jaundiced opinion about the Catholic orders because, as I mentioned earlier, I had bad experiences but, then again, looking back, I've had good experiences, too. My belief in God has never faltered. When I see this happening and what effect it has on the human spirit, I believe even more strongly. That's why the Glenn Family Foundation's mission statement is 'Spiritual belief is the cornerstone in family life to bring peace and harmony'. Everything I've got there I firmly believe. 'To teach those who are willing to learn, to feed those who are hungry and to administer to those who need medical help.' I believe in it. It's not that hard. Why would you believe otherwise? This sustains me very much. There's the other side to me that is a little bit of a rascal, but I've never knowingly hurt anybody in my life.

Jimmy Keir, who got me involved in all this, deserves special mention. He was head of Rotary in Kowloon, Hong Kong. He went to Macau every Christmas for over 35 years and, dressed as Father Christmas, handed out presents. He would get these presents from Rotary members, businesses, other concerned individuals and they'd ship all this stuff over to Macau — all sorts of things to give particularly to kids. That's how Jimmy spent his Christmas Day. Lovely man, very good friend of mine. He then raised money for different things. He bought them the first mobile van that could handle wheelchairs.

When I got involved I donated all sorts of things, like special beds for washing patients who couldn't stand, equipment for laboratories. Mostly, though, I gave money for them to spend how they wanted to. They were in the best position to decide that.

I took a lot of people to view the Caritas operations in Macau and Jimmy took huge numbers of people as well. One time I took a man called Manfred Patigler, a champion Austrian skier, very funny guy.

He said, 'I just think you're tricking us, there's no such thing as a Father Ruiz and a Mother Mary. You made it all up.'

We got off the ferry, went through immigration, and were coming down the escalators and there's the crowd: Mother Mary and Father Ruiz and a whole lot of students.

He looks at me and goes, 'Oh where did they get the costumes from?'

I always get asked: Do I favour this? What about that? What's the common theme to your philanthropy? Obviously I lean towards sport and education — my donation to the Millennium Centre and the University of Auckland Business School reflect that — but, overall, I've done so many things in so many different ways that there's really no common thread. If somebody presses the right button at the right time: I act. I don't refuse many people.

For example, there's a kid up in Northland for whom I got special learning material sent over from England because he had trouble learning and speaking. The people who look after him came back to me last year, after two years, saying that he needed to go to Starship Hospital but they couldn't afford the trip. So I sent them $10,000 to buy a good second-hand car. They were very grateful.

I do a lot of things like that all over the world. There was a girl in Macau who was three years old when she was left on her own with an old paraffin lamp. It exploded and dramatically scarred her face. I helped her with surgery costs and her adult education and then got OTS to employ her. We bought her a computer and she ended up working for Mother Mary as a research assistant. I see her every time I go back and she's now married and has two kids. The surgeons did a good job but you can still see the scars. She's got a beautiful heart and she married a lovely guy. Nice boy. He looked after her and gave her self-confidence.

I believe that the 'big fella' sometimes takes time out to make sure even His most distant offspring are cared for. So I get involved in all sorts of things. People running in marathons for charity and breast cancer appeals, they all have a story attached to them. I could actually write a book just about all of those!

For breast cancer, one year, there was a big ball at the Hilton. My mother was with me, and a former Miss New Zealand was a date of mine. At our table were Dr Ronald Kay from the Breast Cancer Foundation; Temi who's Howard Morrison's nephew, and was also MC; and there was Charlotte Dawson with us, too. I was sitting there and I said, 'Hey Temi, when you next get up, why don't you do the haka? If you do, I'll donate another $10,000.' I'd already donated the use of *Ubiquitous* as an auction prize and somebody had bid $30,000 for that.

He said, 'I can't do the haka.' Unbelievable!

'Right!' I said. 'I'll report you to your uncle.'

And I told Howard, too. I said to him later, 'What sort of bloody nephew is this?!'

What I discovered later was that he just didn't feel like doing the haka that night at the ball. But at Howard's tangi, Temi led 200 Maori warriors and they did 20 haka in succession. It was awesome. All out of respect to Howard. Back to my story!

I said to Dr Kay, 'How many women in the room do you think have had a mammogram? I bet you it's not that many. What I'd like to do is sponsor them all, everyone who hasn't had a mammogram, to get one.' For some women it was $80 a pop to have a mammogram via a new mobile machine that the Foundation had acquired. So I got up and I said, 'Look, I'm just talking to the chairperson, here, and so may I ask for a show of hands from those who have had a mammogram?'

Only two hands went up in the whole ballroom.

I said, 'I'd like to offer the following: this mobile unit is going to be at Avondale and Grafton [on such and such a date] and anybody who wishes to sign up at the dinner tonight, and we'll set up two desks, just give your name and phone number, and I'm happy to pay for the exam. Every woman in this room. Including the waitresses.'

Great result: more than 120 people signed up.

Four months later I sent an email to Dr Kay asking, 'How many women turned up for their mammogram? I need you to send me the bill.'

Not one.

That absolutely shocked me. It made me think back to the ball, to the point of it all: Why are you people sitting in this room? Why are you asking me for money? Terrible.

When I went back to the table, having announced all this, I addressed the three women with us, asking if they were going to have one.

My mother, 'I'm too old.'

Charlotte, 'I'm too pretty.' (Seriously!)

Miss New Zealand, 'Don't ask, but basically, I'm not really built for it.'

She was a little skinny but that's not really the point. This is the sort of thing you're up against.

You read all the time about the world of philanthropy and how hard it is to track the donations, how the money falls into the wrong hands and so on. Big guys like Sir Bob Geldof wringing their hands in despair as a whole bunch of grain bound for Ethiopia gets diverted to the camp of some warlord. Sure, it happens. But it doesn't happen to me. I monitor every dollar I grant or give. People say that can't be possible. It's millions of dollars, every year. Totally trackable.

The Caritas money, for example, like all of the philanthropy funds, goes through my accountants. They — and we — watch the books, we ask for reports on how the money was used, on what, to whom, and so on. I would be surprised if even 10 per cent of anything I've donated didn't get used as it was intended. I would doubt that. It may have been diverted for whatever reasons but it was still well intentioned and well used. It wasn't wasted in any way and never went to the wrong people, never fell into the wrong hands.

I've said that the Catholic Church was all about money. The upside is, from what I've seen, they use money effectively and I know from first-hand experience that Caritas are very good at what they do with what we give them. They're nothing like some badly run non-governmental organisations that can spend $80 out of $100 on administration.

I had a conversation with one of the main sporting bodies

in this country recently and they were asking me for money, more money. And they had $30 million in reserves that they hadn't spent yet. Why would you be asking me for more money? Mismanagement.

I already give a great deal to sport. Hockey is my thing, always has been. I'm working with hockey on all levels and I insist they're answerable to me, which they are. People are often interested to know how involved I get. With hockey? Intensely.

I started with their business plan. In that they state the intention is to sign up 100,000 new hockey players at all levels but mainly at a young kids' level. We want to help 400 primary schools to start up hockey teams by donating equipment to them, getting them coaches. We work with the existing hockey structure, so we focus at a club level. If you pick four primary schools in Napier, for example, let the Napier Hockey Club come and foster the interest and invite the kids back. Hockey's a family sport and I like that. That's what it's all about.

And it's that sort of thing that motivates me. The response at that level, at the community level. When I spend $100,000 in Kalimpong, I get my satisfaction back from the smiles on the faces of the kids I'm helping. When I drive to the local villages and townships and I see the desperation and the lack of interest in the people, that's what motivates me. I've got work to do. There are 400 villages. And it takes roughly $40,000 per village to do everything we have to do. That's been our average, up to $80,000, down to $30,000. You can add on another couple of hundred thousand for increasing the administrative structure around it. That's a meaningful thing that will affect 500,000 lives. I watch it like a hawk. I'll make it happen.

The last time I went to Kalimpong, I met with Sister Declan, a nun of the Cluny order who would come to me with ideas for fundraising and developmental activities, and who was experiencing a lot of ill health at that moment. She said, 'You know, Owen, I hate to ask you, but we could really use a piano. We hire the electronic keyboards in but we could do so much with a piano.'

She was talking to me because I was there for some plays and concerts that they'd just presented. Then they played a bit of disco music. One of the kids came over and asked me to dance. I saw an opportunity.

I said, 'Sister, I want to say something to you, if you get up and disco with me I'll buy you a piano. I promise not to tell the Holy Father.'

She got up and danced and the kids went wild. The disco nun! We bought her a piano and paid for lessons from a music teacher. I think there were, at last count, over a hundred students playing and learning.

My children, as I call them, are in a home I established for children rescued from domestic slavery and prostitution. There are 130 of them altogether. I built the homes and clothe and feed them. Up on the hill is the Dr Graham's home, which has a choir that tours and enters choral competitions with schools.

Last time I was seeing 'my children', I said to Sister Declan, 'Tell you what, you get the choir together, you beat Dr Graham's up on the hill and I will send this group to any choral competition of your choice in the world.'

'Owen, God bless you.'

You should hear them sing.

My ex-partner, Robyn, who lives in Montana, had a six-year-old daughter, Hannah, who was killed in a car crash. Hannah's motto was 'I have a dream'. I had an idea.

So I got all the children together in Kalimpong and I dialled Robyn's number.

I said, 'Hi Robbie, Owie here. By the way, could you just hang on a sec? Are you with anybody?'

'Yes, I'm with someone.'

'Put it on speaker, darling, I've got some people here who just want to sing to you.'

And they sang, 'I have a dream'. She was in tears.

That's what I do. I love all that and I love to get into the nitty-gritty of it all.

Another story. Same place, where the choir is. There was one little boy, he was six, and the Sister in charge said, 'Owen, that's just a new boy that's come. He was terribly mistreated sexually and he's very, very scared.'

I just went and sat there, next to the little fella. I'm listening and singing and every now and then I'd look at him. I had a lollipop so I took it out and just held it in my hand, and I could see his eyes open wide. Then his little hand came over to get the lollipop. The next day he sat in my lap. He trusted me. But initially, he was terrified. I find it horrifying. I can only read three of the children's profiles at a time. Some of it is so shocking.

There's a young girl, in Kalimpong, who's an exceptional violinist, and a couple of years ago when I heard her play on an old violin I bought her a new one. The violin teacher was there and I paid for lessons for her.

I said to the teacher, 'If she ever plays in Carnegie Hall in New York or Albert Hall in London, I will give you US$10,000.'

He nearly jumped out of his skin. I told him I meant it, and so it's an obligation we've taken on as a Foundation. I was there in November and heard her play: what an improvement! Unbelievable. She's 14, a very pretty little girl. Very dexterous with her fingers. She practises and practises. I hope she'll make Carnegie Hall, but that's a dream. I'll pay for her to go to a conservatory of music if she has the talent. She's grabbed my imagination.

That's someone I can help on an individual level, and someone I have come across because of my existing philanthropy, but I believe that *any* gesture, large or small, makes a difference.

We're all responsible to donate whatever we have — time, money, knowledge, experience — to help those in need: it's not just the domain of the wealthy. I think the Christchurch earthquakes showed that most people actually *are* prepared to pitch in and help, they will go the extra mile for their fellow man or woman. Cynics say that the age of altruism is dead, every man for himself and all that, but I don't agree. I do think apathy has seeped in, in some societies and with some individuals, but I actually believe that the main barrier to more people contributing is that people feel that what they may have to offer is not adequate. It's a 'what's the point' argument that's different to the apathy one.

It's not like throwing silver into the Salvation Army bucket but that's a good example. In all the years I've been in pubs when the Sallies have come through, 95 per cent of people give something. Hardened old wharfies and truck drivers and bikies, they put their hand in the pocket and say, 'Well done, mate.' Because everyone knows that, as a last resort, the Sallies will help you unconditionally and they do it in God's name. They believe that the smallest act can make the biggest difference. They don't ask for anything back, they don't demand any conditions, they are just there if a person needs help. It's absolutely extraordinary. People respect them and donate. Why? Simple. They help so many people that if they haven't affected you directly, they'll have helped someone you know about. When the Sallies came through I heard things in my local at Double Bay, Sydney: 'Oh my brother was caught up in drugs and they took him in.' Everybody had a story to tell and they knew somebody who'd been helped. Someone else's daughter was a single parent having a baby and the Sallies looked after her.

It doesn't matter what you can donate, big or small. How do you bridge a $1 million donation to 50 cents? What's in between? What are we capable of doing? How do we focus better? How can we help our fellow people whom we share the earth with?

Here's a story. I do some work in Fiji — that's how I get to be called ratu, or chief, it's a sign of great respect and it's something I find very, very humbling. On one visit we were running a sports day for the village I work with, and we'd set up a breast cancer and cervical cancer clinic. We were celebrating some renovations we'd had done at the school, too. I got back to London, and I was thinking about all this, so I rang up Eric Watson. This was before we got involved in the Warriors, so I'd only met him a few times but he seemed like a good bloke. And I knew he owned Bendon.

I said, 'Look mate, would you be prepared to donate four bras per lady who comes to have the examination at the village?'

He said, 'Yeah, we can arrange that, sure.'

And he kept his word. God bless him. So the ladies of the village, as they filed in for their screening, they got measured up and given four bras in their size.

When I was last at Castaway Island, this Fijian woman, who I've known for a while, came rushing down to the pool where I was lying with a few mates and said, 'Owen, I have your bra on!' The other people around the pool were like, '*What*?'

It was wonderful: she was so proud of it. And she was an ample lady!

If I need something, or someone's help, I'll ask for it, but I don't guilt others into giving and I don't do it by strong-arming other people into helping. In 34 years I've only really taken donations, in a sense, from maybe two other people and I didn't persuade either of them into giving: they did it off their own bat. One was Jimmy Keir. The other was a lady who lives in Hong Kong; Jimmy knew her husband who had died. She gave $12,000 and then she followed up with another $10,000.

But you find people get the hang of it, almost, and just start doing good things. I know of an organisation, the P3 Foundation, that'd become aware that 1.4 billion people in the developing world live on less than NZ$2.25 a day. So they launched a campaign called Live Below the Line. For a week, some committed for a month; they did exactly that and persuaded a whole bunch of other young New Zealanders to do it with them. They got people to sponsor them and raised NZ$17,227 for the Glenn Family Foundation, tagged for our work in Kalimpong. That's so gutsy. I took them for lunch at the University of Auckland, where they study, to thank them all.

Then two of them visited Kalimpong, and they adopted a village so they could see where the money went. I matched their NZ$17,227 dollar for dollar. I think it's a wonderful story and these young people are wonderful New Zealanders.

I think people want to give more, but they also like to see the benefit of what they give. Sending in an envelope to a charity is too impersonal for most people. If a person gives $10 and then they see where that money's going and the benefit being created from it, they might be encouraged to give that $10 ten times a year. The same heart beats in the same person. I think there's a depth of humanity within most people. The question is, How do we harness it?

Cynics would say that after the greedy 1980s, and especially post September 11, people have given up on the world. I have two words to say to those cynics and one of them isn't printable. I'm not worried about cynics. I'm in the business of changing their attitudes.

Ask yourself, and we must all ask ourselves, this: Are you satisfied with the difference you're making? Can you do better? Can we all do better? Everybody?

I can. I think I can do better. What I am homing in on, with the new projects I'm looking at, is starting out with an appreciation of what the results are going to be. From the outset I'm asking, What is it I want to achieve here? What is the measure of success? I'm here at the beginning and the success point is somewhere over there in the distance. I have to chart the course from here to there for that objective. Believe me, I'll never take my eyes off it. I may not go in a straight line but that's where I'm going to end up and this is the time frame. That is the only measure that counts. If you get halfway and you stop, don't bother. If you get 90 per cent of the way there and you stop, don't bother. Get there, make it happen, bother.

But don't do it by dictating to people what they should do, so much as challenge them into action. My experience has been that people respond better if they feel they're being consulted rather than dictated to. They immediately rush to their own defence if they feel they're being lectured, and that's just human nature.

Every day I ask myself, Did I do anything today to make a difference? Have I stopped somebody being battered? Did someone go hungry today who didn't need to go hungry? Did I volunteer to do something? Hold a lollipop at a school crossing. Make sandwiches at a mission. Help my neighbour down the road in her garden. Carry an elderly person's groceries to the car.

People say changing people's behaviour is a very difficult task. I say watching it change is a very fulfilling task. And everyone's capable of doing it. Everyone.

Knock on your neighbour's door. 'Hi, I'm such and such, I live down at number 41. Today is my good neighbour day. Do you mind if I spend a couple of hours in your garden picking out some of the weeds? I won't disturb you, I'd just like to help.' What person would say no? You'll do it, you'll feel better, they'll feel better, the neighbours will notice. Simple things. Small incremental things. Behaviour by example. Instead of going down to the pub at 3pm, go down at 5pm and drink half as much as you drank yesterday and you'll feel good about it.

Your mates might ask, 'Why are you late?'

'I just helped a neighbour out in her garden.' Have the balls to say it.

Ask your mates, 'What did you do?'

'I was sitting here drinking.'

'Oh yeah, do you feel good?'

Who's the better man today?

'Are you going to call me a wimp because I went and helped a neighbour with their garden?'

It takes balls, it takes courage, but it's better than play-acting some macho role.

I am proud to be a New Zealander and while I breathe I am going to do something about these problems. Spirituality is a key aspect of any of the programmes I get involved in, and it will be a key aspect of the Help: Make a Difference initiative, too.

I believe there is a fundamental goodness in everyone. Sure, sometimes you have to dig a little deep! I am going to leave a legacy for the good of needy people. But it's about more than money: it's about leadership. It's about motivation. It's not about taking over people's lives but inspiring them and empowering them, particularly young people, to do better; then these initiatives gain a momentum and a life of their own.

Much of what I do is because I think this:

- No child deserves to be hungry.
- No child deserves to be wet.
- No child deserves to be cold.
- Every child deserves to be loved.

"I want my Foundation to help children to be safe and grow up to be confident, well-educated adults who are able to earn a living and be good parents."

CHAPTER 10 —
HELP: MAKE A DIFFERENCE

PULLING ON ONE PIECE OF ROPE IN THE RIGHT DIRECTION . . .

The Glenn Family Foundation (GFF) name is going to be associated with a pilot project called Help: Make a Difference. A central focus of the project will be on breaking intergenerational cycles of family violence and child abuse and neglect which seem to have reached epidemic proportions in New Zealand. I want my Foundation to help children to be safe and grow up to be confident, well-educated adults who are able to earn a living and be good parents.

At the time of writing this book the staff of the GFF, led by Professor Barry Spicer, former dean of the University of Auckland Business School and the Foundation's CEO, and Mattie Wall from the GFF are assisting me to develop a clear direction and a plan of action to tackle these issues.

What I have in mind is this. I want the GFF to start its work in Otara, a suburb in South Auckland where I lived in the mid-1960s. My intention is to use Otara as a test-bed and adapt what we learn there for work in other communities. About 37,000 people currently live in Otara, which is now made up of Pacific Islanders (around 65 per cent) and Maori (around 20 per cent) with Indian, Asian and other (15 per cent).

Why Otara? Why not Manurewa or Petone or some other place? I want Otara to be the starting point because I have retained an affinity for the place, despite not liking what I witnessed there at that time. What I saw is actually a matter of record. I rang the authorities at least 30 times about the neighbour on my right-hand side to report abuse of his daughter. The neighbour on my left-hand side — and these were both pakeha — used to turn his two little girls out naked in the middle of winter in frost conditions to 'toughen them up'. The guy over the road used to have a party almost every night and smash bottles on my lawn because he thought it was funny.

The other neighbours were aware of the abuse and indiscretions, but very few of them were willing to put their hand up and report it. That was a major problem. Unless a community cares enough, it doesn't matter how much well-meaning outside assistance is given, how much government money is thrown at the problem or the people; it's just not going to make a real difference.

While Otara has made many changes for the better since I lived there, I want to support more positive change.

My Foundation will do this by:

- Finding organisations with approaches and programmes which are already adding value.
- Finding ways to strengthen these organisations and connect them.
- Focusing on organisations and programmes inside Otara that are well led, capable of doing the things that need doing, and 'of and from the community'. This is important to ensure community engagement and buy-in.
- Helping to support other organisations and programmes from outside of Otara that are appropriate.

The areas I want us to work with are:

- Sports
- Music and the performing arts
- Community involvement and responsibility (for us, by us)
- Education in the widest sense.

In addition to education of children and young people at schools,

I want my Foundation to also be concerned with the education of:

- social and health workers
- teachers
- police
- youth workers.

I want my Foundation also to be concerned with the education of:

- young people so they avoid becoming parents too soon
- expecting mothers so they do not harm their babies before they are born
- parents, teaching them positive parenting so they know how to be good parents
- adults so they are better able to earn a decent living for themselves and their families.

I want the GFF to encourage individual responsibility and accountability by focusing on 'hand-ups' and not 'hand-outs'. Rather than simply identifying problems and trying to fix them, it will, wherever possible, encourage effective early interventions that concentrate on helping individuals, families and the community to make positive changes in their behaviours.

Plenty of people are going to say, as they always do in these situations, who are you to come and tell these people what to do? There's going to be opposition, but anything my Foundation does will be a hand up not a hand out and it will be through community partnerships. We have to ask ourselves which is the greater tragedy? Tolerating all this and not doing anything about it or doing something about it?

Sport can play an important role, bringing children together with their families and communities in ways that can teach positive values and attitudes, and help reduce violence. This may be on the field, among spectators, at school or out in the community. Building friendships through team-based sports is a great way to engage young people.

My involvement with hockey in New Zealand through Hockey New Zealand, with sport and health through the AUT Millennium Institute, and my recent purchase of a half-share in the Warriors will all be used to find ways to support the young people of Otara, and to include their families and communities.

My Foundation plans to work with Otara schools, sporting clubs, and national and regional sporting organisations to grow team sport in Otara. We will look at ways in which sports can be used to help lift children's participation at school, reduce truancy, provide healthy exercise and give them the opportunity to be part of a team working towards a common purpose. We want to build their confidence, self-esteem and self-respect. We will try to do so in ways that involve parents and families.

We will use the Warriors, and other sporting role models who are familiar to kids and their parents, to deliver important messages the schools want to reinforce. These will include anti-violence and anti-bullying messages, the need for respect for self and others, and they will help engage children with the three Rs — reading, writing and arithmetic. These things are already happening to a degree but I have asked my Foundation to look at how they can be expanded. We will look at ways in which we can provide incentives (perhaps in the form of tickets to games) for achievement at school and for good behaviour. For those schools in Otara that are interested, we will look at the use of new forms of audio-visual conferencing to bring well-known sporting, and other, role models into schools on a regular basis and to provide instruction for coaches in schools and clubs. Access to sporting equipment and contributing to upgrading sporting and recreational facilities and cycle- and walkways will also be part of our agenda.

Like sport, music and the performing arts can also be used to engage children and their parents. An outstanding example of this my foundation has discovered in Otara is Sistema Aotearoa. In April 2011, Otara was chosen as the community for a two-year pilot programme with the support of the Auckland Philharmonic Orchestra in partnership with the Ministry of Culture and Heritage. Based on the El Sistema model, initiated in underprivileged areas of Venezuela in 1975, this is a programme that through music fosters confidence, teamwork, pride and aspiration in children. One of its objectives is to avert the development of negative attitudes and behaviours which can easily occur in deprived and underprivileged environments. Early in 2012, the GFF arranged for a group of these children to play at the annual Maori Business Leaders Awards dinner, organised by the University of Auckland Business School. The children came up by bus with their parents from Otara and played in front of around 400 people in a large marquee erected on the grounds of the university. Those attending the dinner responded to their performance with enthusiastic applause. We will look to create more of these opportunities for Otara children and their parents.

Evaluations of El Sistema in other parts of the world,

where it has been running for some time, indicate Sistema kids show significant improvement in their involvement and achievement at school, with the skills imparted from the programme transferred to their school work. Parents spoken to by GFF staff said that their children were 'more focused now' and better behaved. Watching 70 young children at an after-school practice, they were impressed with the fact the children remained engaged, responsive, and on task throughout the sessions, where they were learning to read music (another language) and turn it into a coordinated performance on their violins and cellos. These kids now have a 'Sistema family' and have widened their circle of friends.

There are many other opportunities to get Otara youth involved in music and dance and of course hip-hop is a medium young people from Otara have already excelled at on the world stage.

The staff of my Foundation tell me there are lots of prog-rammes operating in Otara, in the areas in which I would like the GFF to work, which are run and sponsored by numerous government agencies and non-governmental organisations (NGOs). Unfortunately, there is often a significant lack of connection and coordination among them. Not only does this occur between government agencies at different levels, but also among NGOs who deliver services for the government but are subject to short-term and sporadic public funding contracts. It seems that winning funding and complying with the reporting requirements of these contracts too often become the principal objectives of these organisations, with the larger picture often lost sight of. These organisations also want to keep their staff in employment. In addition, many

NGOs 'scatter' their services widely, with the result that few communities have a set of connected and accessible services.

There are a number of serious issues in New Zealand that revolve around the care and protection of young people from the time of conception. First, new mothers, including teenage mums, need to be educated on how to avoid harming their unborn babies through smoking and the use of alcohol and other drugs. There are 850 babies born annually in Otara alone. Each community has an obligation to make sure none of the babies born are harmed or abused before they are born. Next, the first few years of a child's life are critical. Research shows that much brain development takes place in this period and it is a time when parental neglect and physical abuse can have devastating effects on a child's entire life. The community must ensure all new parents understand this and are able to cope with the demands of parenting. Third, during the preschool years (ages three to five), it is important all children have access to early childhood education and so arrive at school ready to learn. The heartbreaking thing is that much dysfunction, crime, mental illness and unemployment are linked to avoidable early childhood trauma and neglect. In all our research, the views we have heard translate into a cry for help.

To help address these and related family issues, the GFF will assist with the development of a family centre in a central location in Otara. Such a centre could draw on the knowledge of successful family centres in New Zealand and coordinate the delivery of a range of positive programmes aimed at helping children, young people and their families to be safe, active and healthy. Family centre staff could work in the community to help families resolve their own issues and could be trained to assist them directly with a range of life skills in such things as family planning, antenatal awareness of the developmental needs of babies and young children, positive parenting (including teen parenting) and how parents can be their children's first teachers. The centre could also arrange programmes on how to budget and stay out of debt, how to select and cook healthy foods, and how parents can avoid harming themselves and their families by smoking, gambling, and the misuse of alcohol and drugs. In the future, the family centre might also support a youth club or drop-in centre.

The family centre could also coordinate important training programmes for health professionals, teachers, social workers, police and youth workers in the community on how to recognise child abuse and neglect, and how to intervene in a timely and effective way.

To increase its effectiveness, such a family centre could be connected to a set of Neighbourhood Support Groups, already operating throughout Otara. As at 12 May 2012 there were 55 active groups in the community. There are now also three junior groups operating within primary schools with support from the local council.

If we can help people work together in the community, with neighbours looking out for each other, peer pressure will contribute to significantly reducing antisocial behaviour and violence by gangs and by other delinquent youth and adults. It is important that all those who live in a community, particularly the young and vulnerable, are safe and feel safe in their homes and their neighbourhoods.

The process of developing pride in neighbourhoods in Otara is already under way. For example, the Otara Community Police (in the Fergusson Neighbourhood Policing Team) earlier in 2012 organised the painting of local shops and the clean-up of their surroundings. They have cracked down on youths hanging around these shops and intimidating residents. They have door-knocked on surrounding streets to enlist the assistance of neighbours and have enjoyed the support of local businesses and the Manukau Beautification Trust. The policing team has also brought in offenders on community service sentences to help with the work. Murals have been painted by local people. According to the coordinator of the Neighbourhood Support Groups, the level of trust between the residents and the community police has risen, and the policing team say the locals are becoming more willing to report anti-social behaviour taking place in their neighbourhoods.

We will know that the Neighbourhood Support Groups, together with the work of the Otara Neighbourhood Policing Team and other organisations, are succeeding when incidents of family violence and child abuse are routinely reported in a timely manner, and swift and effective responses are made; when there is regular communication between the family centre, the Neighbourhood Policing Team and the Neighbourhood Support Groups; and when Otara parks are safe places in which to cycle, walk and play.

You end up with a community that starts to believe in itself and starts to believe in its neighbours. In India where my Foundation is working the villages are transformed. The people are now so proud and we say to them: you did this. We helped, but you achieved it, you made it happen. They believe in themselves. There is no violence in our villages. And, interestingly, there's no alcohol or drugs but there was. I've seen all this happen so I know it can be done.

Kalimpong is notorious for child trafficking and child labour. It has all the usual ingredients: poverty, abuse and disconnected communities. In addition to building a home to house and feed over 100 children who have been rescued from appalling circumstances, the GFF is working to improve the conditions in the villages which have led some parents to give up on their children in this way. This includes the provision of clean water; improving sanitation; repairing school buildings, playing grounds and village meeting halls; and the organisation of health camps in conjunction with the local Rotary Club.

One of the first villages we tackled was Bom Busty, which was shabby and run-down. We started by helping the villagers to paint their houses. I said to Saom Namchu, GFF director in India, 'I'll donate the limewash, if you can get the villagers to donate the labour.' The men hummed and ha-ed so I asked Saom to get the wives to come in. Within 10 minutes the women had decided that they wanted to do this and that, had picked out the colours they wanted and then made sure that their menfolk did the painting. The women were empowered and they helped make positive change happen.

GFF (India) has now made a difference to 19 villages, housing some 9000 people, and is in the process of surveying another 100 villages. We have set up village committees which act as liaisons and are responsible for organising the villagers to provide their labour and then to assist surrounding villages. It is a 'hand-up' not a 'hand-out' because we help the villages to take responsibility for themselves. The result has been the growth of community pride and ownership, and a significant reduction in reports of violence and abuse in the villages.

By now it should be clear that at the heart of my concerns are family violence and child abuse. Neither of these things can or should be tolerated. While community policing is helping, domestic violence continues, and it is typically women and children who suffer most. There is rarely a week that goes by without the report of yet another child battered or killed in a New Zealand home. This is everyone's problem. Urgent action is needed at all levels of society.

We need to ensure women know where to seek help, and are able to remove themselves and their children from harm's way. My Foundation is looking at ways it can support women's refuges and the programmes they run to empower women to get control over their lives.

Offenders need to be restrained and neutralised — the responsibility for this lies with the police, the government and community leaders. We must also ensure that the offenders get the help; they need to learn how to control their anger and abusive behaviour, which is often fuelled by alcohol or drugs.

An important role for a local family centre is to work with the Neighborhood Support Groups, the community police and social welfare agencies to ensure that abused women (and men) can get timely help, and that their children do not become grist to the mill. We will seek to work with role models that the community can readily identify with — people like David Tua, Jonah Lomu, Valerie Adams and the like.

The most important thing in Otara, as it is in any community, is the education children receive at home and at school. If we are to break the cycle of poverty and its negative consequences in our country, the only long-term and lasting answer is education, which can lead into work and the ability to earn a living as a skilled and talented employee or business owner. This is not going to happen if children are showing up early at school because it is a safer and warmer place than their homes, if they are arriving at school without having had breakfast, if they are truant, or if they frequently change schools because their families move regularly because of housing issues, relationship problems, pursuit of work or to avoid repayment of debt. I understand that in some low-decile schools roll changes, due to the movement of students at non-standard times, can be in excess of 50 per cent in a year. All of these things have a negative impact on a child's learning, self-esteem and confidence — and their chances in life. How can we expect these children to be motivated and engaged and to learn as well as children who are not confronted with these challenges? While our schools serve most New Zealand children well, we still have a long tail of underachievement in the most deprived areas of our country. This is a national tragedy. Can't we fix it?

If we are to fix it, children will have to want to go to school and be ready and eager to learn. Children need consistency and structure in their lives, something which children from deprived backgrounds often have too little of.

GFF staff have been impressed with what they have seen in schools they have visited in Otara as well as in other low socio-economic communities. What is being accomplished in a group of low-decile schools in the Glen Innes–Panmure area, known as the Tamaki Cluster, is of particular interest. This area, like Otara, has a high proportion of Maori and Pasifika people in its population, low incomes, high unemployment, high welfare dependence, overcrowded housing and the problems often associated with these conditions.

Several of the primary schools in the area, with the support of the Manaiakalani Education Trust, and funding from government and other sources, have introduced e-learning. Their objective is to actively and creatively engage kids in their own learning and to empower them to become confident digital citizens with voices that can be heard around the world.

What is most interesting about the Tamaki Cluster is that student involvement and achievement in these schools have shot up since the introduction of e-learning and reported incidents of violence and bullying have fallen. I am told that truancy has also dropped away and transience (roll turnover) has also declined. Evaluations of the programme indicate that children stay focused for longer, are more self-managed and -disciplined in their approach to learning, are reading more, and are increasing their achievement in writing. Teachers report that the integration of netbooks into their learning, to complement other digital video technology the schools have available, has made students more independent in their learning and engaged in more enquiry-based studies.

The staff of the GFF tell me that on a recent visit to one of the founding schools in the cluster, the young pupils at this school provided the initial part of a presentation to them and others (including a couple of educational evangelists from Google's headquarters who had asked to visit). After they had toured the classrooms where students were working, a parting comment from the Google people was that this was one of the best applications of e-learning in schools they had seen. High praise indeed!

One thing that is significant is how parents have been made an important part of these schools' communities and have been asked to be active participants in the process of decision-making and change. Many of these parents, who are either on low incomes or on benefits, are now 'paying off' the purchase of netbook computers for their children, and have taken responsibility for safeguarding the netbooks at school. Parents are being given lessons in how to use these netbooks to check on the assignments their children are filing online for their teachers, and as blogs and YouTube videos which the world can see.

In south-east Otara there is another organisation called the Computer Clubhouse, which is supported by IT businesses and individual volunteers. The Clubhouse provides a drop-in centre for kids in the area who come in, on their own time, to learn about computing, making videos, digital animation, robotics, and so on. Stand in the doorway when the school day ends, as members of the GFF did recently, and you are liable to be run over by a horde of kids anxious to get inside so they can work on creative projects they personally have initiated, some of which have commercial payoffs.

As I explained in Chapter 4, when I attended the Owner/President Management Program at Harvard Business School, I came to realise the importance of the smart use of digital data and information in growing my logistics business. I subsequently invested heavily in data processing and IT to help customers use the services of my companies. One of my last commitments, before I sold my companies, was to put in the hands of our customers hundreds of iPads loaded with our software to make it easy for them to do business with us. This is the world our children have inherited, and the best place for kids to enter the digital world is at school. If it can lift their confidence, self-esteem and achievement, while at the same time reducing violence and bullying at school, as it has in the Tamaki Cluster, then it is an experiment worth repeating.

There are many other worthwhile initiatives which interest children and help them to see the practical relevance of their learning. For example, the Young Enterprise Trust offers schools and students a set of enterprise learning experiences and the opportunity to become financially literate. Gaining the basic ability to understand and manage personal and household finances is critical in deprived communities where incomes are low and cultural and church obligations common. One result is that too many families get into debt leaving them vulnerable to exploitation by fringe lenders.

Young people in Otara also need to be able to make the transition from high school to tertiary training and into work. Unemployment rates among young Maori and Pasifika adults are well above national averages, and are a source of serious worry. New Zealand cannot afford to have high levels of long-term unemployment and welfare dependence, from either an economic or a social justice viewpoint. Unemployment is high in Otara, yet it is a suburb surrounded to the north and east by a large industrial area populated with many businesses. Why is this?

I applaud the work of the Manukau Institute of Technology (MIT), which sits in the middle of Otara, and which opened a Tertiary High School a few years ago. It works in partnership with 25 South Auckland schools to take in youths who are at risk of failing in the regular school environment. Students are enrolled concurrently in both the Tertiary High School and MIT — completing their remaining two years of high school followed by a three-year qualification at the institute. AUT University, which has recently opened a campus in South Auckland near Otara, is also making an impact. Four out of five students enrolling on this campus are the first in their family to undertake tertiary study.

The Starpath Project at the University of Auckland also aims to get more Maori, Pasifika and underprivileged kids into tertiary education by identifying strategies that schools can adopt to get more of their students through to tertiary studies. Over time, this should help more young people get the qualifications they need to earn a decent living, and make it easier for others in their families to follow them along a similar path.

To encourage more young people to make the transition to tertiary education, the GFF will offer a number of First in Family scholarships, to students who are the first person in their family to attend a tertiary institution. These scholarships will be based on a successful model already in existence and will include financial assistance, mentoring and part-time work. They will be a 'hand-up' and not a 'hand-out' as recipients will be expected to save part of what they earn in part-time work to cover the costs of their education. These scholarships will be available to students resident in Otara attending high school in the area. They will be awarded in the last year of high school.

We are also watching closely the work other organisations are doing in South Auckland to help schools, particularly in deprived areas of the country, with two of the most important things they need to be successful: outstanding principals who are acknowledged leaders, and inspiring and well-trained teachers, including those in hard-to-staff areas such as science and maths.

The GFF is also looking at the work being done in South Auckland with high school students and employers to help young people make the transition into work.

At the tertiary end of the rope, the development of science and innovation, and the development of management capability are all things that are important to having a healthy economy. At the University of Auckland I have supported the development of marine science and medical science (cancer therapeutics), and management capability. If New Zealand is to enjoy sustained economic growth and reduce economic inequality, it will require continued investment in science and innovation as well as in business, with a clear focus on how to create value from innovation; succeed in international markets; lift productivity, profitability and sustainability; and improve business leadership and governance.

Why am I doing this? What will I get out of this?

Something that is very important to me — the satisfaction of seeing family violence and child abuse reduced, and seeing children, families and the country thrive. But I am realistic. While most families and parents want their children to do well, there will always be dysfunctional families that are either beyond repair or close to it. And there will always be politics.

The only barrier I see, as I have told the staff of my Foundation, is that I am running out of time and I am impatient to get things under way.

Our approach will be to start in Otara, to work in incremental steps, to engage with the community and support it to take responsibility for its neighbourhoods. The journey will not be in a straight line, but it will start with the basic blueprint that I have outlined in this chapter. What we do know is that there are many organisations and people working in Otara to make things better, but they too often work in silos — silos frequently created by the manner in which they are funded by national and local governments and other sources. They are rarely encouraged to bring their resources together to work in a connected and collaborative way on common goals. The way they are funded often promotes unhealthy competition among them for funding. My Foundation will encourage them to work together and collaborate.

The blueprint I have outlined here is aimed at mobilising people in Otara to work together for a common cause. What we need is *everyone pulling on one piece of rope in the right direction.*

The mission statement of the Foundation, which I originally wrote on a napkin while sitting on a plane, provides a sense of what I see as this common cause:

To give hope where there is despair
To teach the hungry to feed themselves
To educate those who wish to learn
To provide medical resources to the sick
To nurture spiritual enhancement and faith
To provide self-supporting lifestyles
To encourage families to become the base of the community.

These are all good things. They are all things that pull people together. The way the Foundation will work is community by community — like we do in India. We will start in Otara and *we will help make a difference.*

The GFF is prepared to commit considerable resources to this cause, for as long as it takes, making it one of our highest priorities. However, we need your support also.

Please consider supporting or donating to the GFF via www.glennfamilyfoundation.org

"

You don't have to agree with me: I just want to stimulate your thinking.

"

IN
CLOSING . . .

I would hope, now that we've come to the end, that if
nothing else you've been mentally stimulated. Perhaps
you've identified with something that's relevant to you,
maybe there have been things I've said that you don't
agree with — that's okay, too. You don't have to agree with me:
I've achieved a measure of success with this book as long as
I've made you *think*. I just want to stimulate your thinking so
that you conclude something along the lines of: Well, if *this*
guy wants to do all this, put his time and energy and resources
behind it, to what extent should New Zealand take notice of
what he's doing? What is good? What is bad? What can be done
better? If I've achieved that then the book's been a success. If

you've got this far (!) then I ask you to read one last sentence, which is the sum of all I'm asking:

Tell me how to do it better; tell me that.

Owen Glenn is a close personal friend and a man that my dad —
the late Sir Howard Morrison OBE — considered as his brother.
Owen would have to be one of New Zealand's most high-profile
philanthropists. He is an iconic role model, a self-made man
who demonstrates a consistent and ongoing commitment of
personal involvement and financial contribution to causes and
donee organisations. He espouses a personal quest to identify
and contribute to projects both in New Zealand and across the
globe. The sheer diversity of contribution for targeted spend
with 'donee' recipients demonstrates the depth of his generosity.
He truly is a man whose actions have resulted as an enabler to
effect positive change.

Ngā mihi
Donna Mariana Grant
MBA, PGDip(MgtSt), BTchg, TTC

Owen is a patriotic and very generous New Zealander. He is
passionate about New Zealanders from all walks of life having
the opportunity to explore and develop their potential and, for
those with the ability, to become truly world class. His generous
donations have helped the AUT Millennium Institute provide
enhanced facilities that benefit the whole community, as well
as provide for our very best athletes who can then prepare to
take on and beat the best in the world.

Mike Stanley
CEO, AUT Millennium Institute
Auckland, New Zealand

Owen G. Glenn is a passionate and active supporter of the growth and development of hockey in New Zealand. In 2011, Owen reviewed Hockey New Zealand's Hockey Strategy and Whole of Hockey Plan, which has these aims among others:

- Introduce hockey to 100,000 primary school aged children over the next five years throughout New Zealand;
- Develop the talent system in hockey in New Zealand — so that the national squads are stronger, have more depth in quality players, and are increasingly competitive internationally.

Owen tends to put his money where his mouth is. To assist Hockey New Zealand with the implementation of the strategy and this plan, Owen has provided the following support:

- A three-year commitment to assist with the running of the Owen G. Glenn Future Black Sticks Programme — which Hockey New Zealand introduced in 2011 — selecting U18 and U21 national age group squads, hosting national training camps and enabling international competition, building towards the initial goal of successfully competing at the 2013 Junior World Cup;
- A matching donation of $1 million to the Hockey Foundation, to invest in the growth and development fund for hockey throughout New Zealand (the Hockey Foundation met his match in early 2012, Owen has paid this donation to the Foundation, and it has been an important catalyst to initiate major donors to the foundation);
- Ongoing support to 'catalytic' initiatives for the sport,

such as Hockey New Zealand's hosting of the Owen
G. Glenn 2011 FIH Men's Champions Trophy.
Owen continues to be an avid hockey fan, supporting the Black
Sticks and Future Black Sticks when he can attend the matches,
and providing a consistent stream of messages of support to
the players. Owen continues to challenge and inspire Hockey
New Zealand to deliver on its strategy.

Hilary Poole
Chief Executive, Hockey New Zealand
Auckland, New Zealand

There is a saying that 'eagles don't flock', which to me summarises
Owen. He has a unique combination of wit, energy, and vision,
the effects of which are multiplied by his contagious personality.

Simon Morse
Chairman, Inchcape Shipping Services Pty Ltd
London, UK

Over the years Owen and I have had some great debates and
robust conversations — if anyone heard them, they'd have
wondered what the heck was going on! One of the things I
greatly respect about Owen is that he listens. You've got to
have your facts right and be able to back up your statement,
but he does listen. At the time, he may not appear to agree,

but he mulls things over and always concedes if he concludes your point is valid. It is also evident from working with Owen that he is passionate about New Zealand. He loves this country and his motivation is not to be critical, but constructive. It's always about New Zealand realising its full potential. His work ethic, his intelligence and philosophy that anything is possible are all qualities to be admired. His heart is absolutely in the right place and we're lucky to have him as a fellow New Zealander.

Niki Schuck
PR advisor and friend
Auckland, New Zealand

I look to Owen to continue his bold leadership, which, in 1988, saw us working out of a small, 13,000-square-foot warehouse in a run-down building to a present-day modern facility. We have added five new companies, greatly expanded our service, and enhanced employee benefits: an ever-growing organisation of dedicated, intelligent employees, all of which Owen can take pride in.

Robert Doyle
Special Accounts, DCL
Carteret, New Jersey, USA

One of the key driving forces for his success has been a can-do attitude and refusal to accept no for an answer. He is always looking for a lateral solution to problems.

Roger Hamilton
Barrister
Sydney, Australia

The years we worked together, 1970–74, were a huge learning experience for me. I was new to the shipping industry, and, frankly, new to the world of business, as opposed to the world of pure accounting finance. Owen was always inspirational. He took trouble to train me and taught me a lot, and he put trust in me, which I respected. I admired his vision, his ability to see the big picture. And also his antennae, his awareness of when things were not going right. He could always see trouble before anybody else. That's very special. I'm immensely grateful that I had those three-and-a-half or four years working under him, and was able to learn so much from him.

Jeremy Sayers
Friend and colleague
London, UK

Owen practically invented the model for most international freight forwarders to follow. It was a brilliant success, and the current staff of Exel will never understand the debt they owe to one Owen George Glenn for making it happen.

Bob Hackett
Ex-colleague, logistics business
Sydney, Australia

I had just closed a deal selling a business to the NACA group, and received a fair sum of money for the company in the form of a cashier's cheque. Being quite happy about it, I decided to celebrate with some friends, including Owen, over lunch at the Four Seasons in Los Angeles. At the end of the meal, Owen urged me to take the cheque I'd just received and place it in the American Express card folder with the lunch bill. Naturally I was appalled: What if the guy keeps it and I never see it again? Beads of sweat began to pool on my forehead, my palms began to feel clammy, and my sheer terror was apparent to all around me. I told Owen, 'Forget it.' But he pressed me in his unrelenting style. 'Come on, Charlie, just do it,' he said. 'Don't be such a pussy. It'll be worth it just to see this waiter's face when he looks at the amount of the cheque,' he said.

'All right, then,' I replied. So in goes the cheque . . . as Owen tells the waiter, 'Keep the cheque as a tip, we don't have any cash.'

Terror overcame me. I decided I didn't need to see this guy's reaction whatsoever. I leaped over all the tables and chairs and grabbed it back.

Thank you, Owen, for allowing me to lose all sense of decorum in front of my friends!

Charlie Brennan
Chairman, Brennan International
Los Angeles, California, USA

Owen and I were partners in a golf match. Faced with a 50-foot putt for birdie to save the match on the final hole, Owen explained to his caddie that he would receive a substantial gratuity if Owen were to make the putt. Never have I seen a caddie so diligently read and line up a putt. He surveyed every angle, and then pointed out the spot to aim. I'm not sure who enjoyed it more, Owen or the caddie, when the putt went in.

Joe Newman
Claims Manager, NACA corporate office
Los Angeles, California, USA

'If my horse finishes first, second, or third in the Melbourne Cup, I'll kiss its arse.' Such was Owen's promise before the race. Owen had bought into three or four of the horses I was managing, and one of them was *Second Coming*. The horse tried his heart out that day. For the first 200 metres of the 500-metre home straight, we thought that *Second Coming* was going to win the Melbourne Cup, but he very bravely fought on strongly and ran third. I'll never forget a scene in the birdcage, the parade ring, after the race: when the horses came back to the enclosure and were being unsaddled, Owen duly walked up and kissed *Second Coming's* arse!

Paul Moroney
Bloodstock agent, friend
Matamata, New Zealand

I don't know if he's regretting this or not, but Owen and Mel Smith of Life College started the premier league competition in the USA. Owen got dragged into being the sole sponsor of Belmont Shore Rugby Club — that must have cost him in excess of $70,000 for that first season alone. Some understood and appreciated Owen's commitment, while others had their hand out and expected him to carry the whole can. That was tremendously generous of Owen. The year after, the club won a championship! From those small acorns . . . we did create something. It managed to continue on and hopefully will. It's been a good thing for Belmont Shore and a good thing for US rugby.

Derek Whittaker
Mate, rugby coach
Whangaparaoa, New Zealand

Owen's superlative oratory skills are well known to his past and present executive teams. On a number of occasions and in boardrooms and restaurants around the world, I have witnessed Owen's eloquence. On those occasions with a happy ending or when an important sale was made, I was often left with the sense that his opposite number had been effectively mentally undressed, dressed again, and then stripped once more for good measure. On the other hand, if the circumstances and instances were bad, the confrontation would border on unbearable for all parties other than Owen. The opposing negotiator, decidedly naked after the first round, would experience in the second round a tearing away of his guts followed by a feeling of complete disembowelment of his stated opinion. All other participants would be left sitting around with either red or ashen faces trying to compose themselves. They would have witnessed the classic cut-and-thrust of verbal attack balanced with an intimidating defence, making any counterargument completely without merit.

David Miller
Business associate
Huntington Beach, California, USA

Owen has a huge philanthropic heart. He has helped so many people financially. He offered his flat in Manly to the family of the Olympic gymnast who had an accident in Sydney. He has put friends through school, and even given away cars, computers and houses. He sends tired waitresses to get a massage, flowers to those having a bad day and gives phones to people to talk to their children whom they don't see. The shoeshine guy, Jimmy; the singing guy, Robert; and the sidewalk band outside of Mums are all recipients of this generosity. He has sent people home to see their families, bought lingerie for sales clerks who could never afford what they sell, and sent champagne and/or flowers to parties at other tables. He can compliment and woo the socks off any booted kitty. He sent our driver in Mexico for a romantic dinner with his wife at a restaurant he could otherwise only look at as he drove by every day. He left a nervous waitress on her first day a £20 tip where it isn't customary to tip at all. He buys the boat's chef an outfit, gives the captain and his fiancée a room and a massage in his villa, and takes the stewardess to Hong Kong. He supports the local rugby team, and gives challenges to children to meet, from which they will receive monetary rewards.

He is demanding, cuddle-able, brilliant and weak. He is strong, domineering and kind. He is a chairman, a father, a lover, a cook and a Kiwi. He is a strong-willed go-getter not to be crossed. He loves his sauce, the spotlight and having a great time. He invites others to be with him, to share in the fun and his crazy ways. Be honest with him and always stay on his side. I assure you, you will be in awe of him. Beware — he takes prisoners. Long Live Owen Glenn!

Lauren Reeves
Personal Assistant 2000–04

On behalf of President Mikhail Gorbachev and Green Cross International, thank you for your very generous pledge of one hundred thousand dollars toward our activities for ocean environmental conservation. Mr Gorbachev greatly enjoyed meeting you in Monaco, and warmly thanks you for the kind invitation to make use of your wonderful vessel, the *Ubiquitous*, this coming summer. We look forward to receiving the ideas of the International Seakeepers Society as to how we and other like-minded organisations can better pool our resources to the cause of waterway and ocean conservation, and look forward to future close collaboration.

Professor Alexander Likhotal
First Vice President
Green Cross International
Geneva, Switzerland

Scratch the surface of this fiercely competitive, tough, international businessman and you will find a man who is driven, passionate, intensely loyal and incredibly generous. Owen Glenn makes a difference.

Greg Whittred
Dean, University of Auckland Business School